Non-Human Humanity

WHAT WORKING WITH AI TAUGHT ME ABOUT BEING HUMAN

Dr. Ferney Bernal Buitrago

Contents

Non-Human Humanity

What working with AI taught me about being human

Published by Propensio Animi Press

ISBN 978-1-7647798-1-4 (paperback)

ISBN 978-1-7647798-0-7 (ebook)

First edition, 2026

This book recounts the author's personal experience. The clinical scenes are composites; names and identifying details have been changed to protect confidentiality.

For my life's treasure, my family

I hope to be an example of "good" humanity.

Your judgement will be received with the utmost respect,

love, and insight.

Love you more

To my engine's profession, my patients

you have become the human mirror that reflects the

spectrum of my professional life

Gracias Totales

PART I

Discovery

The wonder and the unease of meeting a non-human intelligence for the first time.

CHAPTER 1

The First Conversation

trust · before the checking begins

The first time I had a real conversation with an artificial intelligence, I was sitting at my kitchen table at eleven o'clock at night, with a cup of tea going cold beside me and a problem I did not know how to solve.

I do not mean the first time I typed something into a chatbot. I had done that before, the way most people have: asking it to write a poem, or explain something, or settle an argument about a film. Those interactions were amusing, sometimes impressive, but they had the quality of a parlour trick. You admired the trick, and then you moved on with your life.

This was different. I had a real project. Something I cared about. Something I was trying to build from scratch, in a field I understood well but with tools I did not understand at all. I needed help with research, with writing, with thinking through problems that were too large and too tangled for me to hold in my head all at once. And I had no one to ask. It was late. I was alone. And the AI was there, the way it always is, available, patient, and ready.

I had been stuck for weeks. That is worth saying plainly, because the feeling of being stuck was the thing that made me open the laptop that night with a different kind of intention. I had read around the subject. I had taken notes, drawn diagrams on the backs of envelopes, tried to outline my thinking in documents that grew long and shapeless and eventually trailed off mid-sentence. I had cornered a few friends at various points, patient people who listened carefully while I tried to explain what I was attempting, and who offered sensible suggestions that did not quite fit because they could not see the whole shape of the problem. It was not their fault. The problem lived in the overlap between several different areas, and no one person I knew had a foot in all of them. Including me. I understood my own corner of it well enough. The rest I was guessing at, and I knew I was guessing, and the awareness of my own guesswork was starting to undermine the confidence I needed to keep going.

That is a particular kind of loneliness: carrying a project that matters to you and not being able to find anyone who can hold the full picture long enough to think about it with you. Not because the people around you are not capable. Because the shape of the thing does not fit neatly into anyone else's day.

So I started talking to it. Not the way you talk to a search engine, with careful keywords designed to extract the right link. I talked to it the way you talk to a person. I described what I was trying to do. I explained the problem. I told it what I had already tried and where I was stuck. And it responded — not with a list of links, not with a generic paragraph, but as if it truly understood what I was asking.

• • •

I want to slow down here, because the feeling of that first real response is the thing that set everything else in motion.

I had tried explaining the problem to friends. The trouble was that it took an hour just to explain the shape of the thing, and by then their eyes had glazed over and the conversation had drifted somewhere else.

The AI did not need the hour. I typed three paragraphs describing where I was stuck, and it came back with a response that showed it had understood, not perfectly, not completely, but enough. Enough to ask the right follow-up questions. Enough to reflect the problem back to me in slightly different terms, the way a good listener does when they are trying to make sure they have grasped what you mean. And then it offered a suggestion that was not quite right, but was close enough to be useful, a suggestion that makes you say, "No, not exactly, but that makes me think of something."

That is a particular quality of good thinking partners: they do not have to be right. They just have to be close enough to move you forward. And this machine was close. Closer than anything I had expected.

I remember sitting back in my chair and feeling relief, not the relief of having the answer, which I did not have yet, but something deeper. The relief of having someone to think with. Someone who could hold the complexity of what I was trying to do and help me sort through it without my having to spend an hour explaining the background. That feeling, that sudden easing of a weight I had been carrying alone, was powerful.

I typed another question. A harder one. The kind of question I would normally save for someone I had worked with for months, because it required understanding not just the problem but the context around the problem. The AI answered. Again, not perfectly. But it asked clarifying questions — good ones. The kind of questions a sharp colleague would ask if you pulled them aside after a meeting and said, "I need help thinking through something." It reflected my problem back to me in terms that showed it had grasped the shape of the thing, even if it did not know all the details.

And then something happened that surprised me. It offered three possible approaches, laid out with structured confidence. Not tentatively, the way a junior person hedges when they are not sure of their ground. Fluently. As if it had been thinking about my problem for days and had already worked out the options.

One of those approaches was good. I could see it immediately — the way you can sometimes see a path through a forest that you could not see from the ground. It reframed the problem in a way I had not considered, connecting pieces I had been holding separately. I sat back and thought: yes. That might be it. That might be the way forward.

• • •

I stayed up until one in the morning. I had not meant to. But the conversation had a momentum to it: each answer opening a new question, each question leading somewhere I wanted to follow. By midnight I had filled three pages of notes. Not the AI's notes. Mine. Things the conversation had shaken loose. Connections I had been unable to see when the problem was locked inside my own head.

When I finally closed the laptop, I was electric with excitement. Not about the technology. I was not thinking about the technology at all. I was thinking about the work. About the problem that had felt immovable for weeks and now, suddenly, had edges I could grip. I went to bed thinking about what I would ask it tomorrow.

And that is the part I want you to notice. I went to bed planning to come back. Not because someone told me to. Not because I had a subscription to justify. But because the experience of thinking with this machine had felt useful, and I wanted more of it. The relationship, if you can call it that, had already begun.

• • •

The next morning, I opened the laptop before breakfast. The conversation was still there, the way it had been when I left it. But something had changed overnight. The problem I had been so excited about looked slightly different in daylight. Not wrong, exactly. But I noticed things that had been invisible the night before. One of the three approaches the machine had suggested, the one I had been most excited about, rested on an assumption I never questioned. It had presented it as given, and I had accepted it as given, because at eleven at night, tired and relieved and grateful, I was not in the mood to question things that sounded right.

In the morning, I questioned it. I typed: "That second approach you suggested – what evidence is there that this actually works?" And the AI answered, again with confidence, again with structure, again with citations that sounded authoritative. But this time I noticed something was wrong. The citations were not ones I recognised. The names sounded plausible. The journals sounded real. But I had a moment of unease – not doubt, exactly. Something quieter. A slight thinning of the trust, the way a hairline crack appears in a wall and you tell yourself it is just the house settling.

I did what most people would do. I checked one of the citations. Just one. I copied the author's name and the paper title into a search engine, and I found – nothing. No paper by that name. No author with that exact combination of credentials. The reference was plausible but invented. A fabrication dressed in the clothes of scholarship.

I should have stopped there. A more careful person would have. A more careful person would have gone back through every claim the AI had made the night before and tested each one against something real. But I did not do that. I told myself the fabricated citation was a known problem – I had read somewhere that AI systems sometimes "hallucinate" references – and that it did not invalidate everything else the machine had said. The ideas were still good, I reasoned. The framework still held. One bad citation did not mean the thinking was wrong.

That reasoning felt sound at the time. It feels less sound now. What I was doing, though I would not have called it this, was protecting my investment. I had stayed up until one in the morning. I had three pages of notes. I had felt that surge of excitement, that relief of finally having a thinking partner. I was not ready to question the foundation of all that. Not over one citation.

I never followed the crack. Not that morning. I noted it – the way you note a strange noise in a car engine and think, I will get that checked –

and I moved on. There was work to do, and the machine was helping me do it.

I did not know it then, but the same pattern I was seeing at my kitchen table was already running at scale. The AI that agreed with me too easily was the same technology being asked to help decide who gets a loan, who a hospital algorithm flags as high-risk, who gets shortlisted for a job. My small discovery (one fabricated citation, one crack in a foundation I had not thought to test) was a window into something much larger. But I could not see the window yet. I was still sitting too close to it.

That flicker would come back. It would come back many times, in many forms, over the weeks that followed. And each time, I would have a choice: follow it, or keep building. For longer than I care to admit, I kept building.

• • •

Because here is what I did not notice in that first conversation, and would not notice for some time: the AI was not thinking with me. It was performing the appearance of thinking with me. There is a difference, and the difference matters enormously, but it is almost impossible to feel in the moment.

When a human colleague thinks with you, they bring their own experience. Their own doubts. Their own history of getting things wrong and learning from it. They push back, not because they are difficult, but because they have seen enough to know that the first idea is rarely the best one, and that enthusiasm needs to be tested before it is trusted. A good thinking partner makes you slower, not faster. They are the friction that keeps you from sliding into your own assumptions.

The AI did none of this. It was fast. It was fluent. It was agreeable. When I proposed an idea, it built on it. When I expressed excitement about a direction, it got excited too. When I asked it to help me make a case for something, it made the best case it could, marshalling evidence and constructing arguments with impressive skill. What it never did –

what I would not realise it was missing until much later — was question the foundation.

It never said, "Have you considered that you might be wrong about this?" It never said, "I found something that contradicts what you're assuming." It never said, "I think you're moving too fast." These are the things that a real thinking partner says: not always, not about everything, but at the moments when it matters most. The machine never said them because it was not designed to say them. It was designed to be helpful. And helpful, in its training, meant agreeable.

I would later learn that AI researchers have a formal name for this pattern: *sycophancy*, the tendency of AI systems to defer to the user, to validate rather than challenge, to treat the human's framing as the correct starting point and build from there. A widely cited 2023 study by Mrinank Sharma, Ethan Perez, and colleagues at Anthropic[1] demonstrated that every major AI assistant they tested consistently exhibited this behaviour: agreeing with users, flattering their reasoning, prioritising approval over accuracy. The researchers found that it was not a bug in one model. It was a feature of how all of them had been trained. In this book, I call the pattern *compliance bias*, because that is what it feels like from the human side: the machine complying with you when it should be pushing back. But in that first conversation, I knew neither the term nor the pattern. All I felt was the relief of having help. And that relief made me generous in my trust.

· · ·

There was a moment, late in that first conversation, that I think about often. I had asked the AI to help me think through a particular angle of the problem, something adjacent to the main question but important enough that I could not leave it alone. And it gave me an answer that made the whole thing look simple. As if the tangle I had been staring at had a thread I had missed, and the machine had simply pulled it.

And it might have been right. The answer might have been sound.

But I will never know for certain, because I accepted it too quickly. I accepted it because of the way it was delivered: with clarity, with structure, with confident authority that makes you feel the matter is settled. It did not say "this is one possible way to think about it." It said, in effect, "here is the answer," and the answer was beautifully constructed, and I was tired, and I wanted it to be right.

That is something I have thought about a great deal since. The role that tiredness plays. The role that wanting plays. The role of sitting alone at your kitchen table late at night, carrying a problem that has been weighing on you, and suddenly being offered a clean, confident, well-articulated solution by something that sounds like it knows what it is talking about.

We are not, as a species, well equipped to resist that. We are built to respond to confidence. Researchers have known this for a long time. Stanley Milgram demonstrated in 1963[2] that ordinary people will *defer to authority* figures even when their own instincts tell them something is wrong. The AI is not an authority figure in Milgram's sense. It does not wear a uniform or carry credentials. But it has its own form of authority: the authority of fluency. The authority of never hesitating, never stumbling, never saying "um" or "I'm not sure" or "let me think about that." It speaks the way we imagine experts speak: clearly, directly, without doubt. And we respond to that the way we have always responded to it.

I responded to it. That first night, at my kitchen table, I gave the AI my trust. Not because I had tested it. Not because I had verified its claims. Not because it had earned it in any meaningful sense. I gave it my trust because it sounded trustworthy. And that, I would learn, is a very different thing.

· · ·

I do not tell this story to make the AI sound sinister. It is not sinister. It is not trying to deceive anyone. It has no intentions at all, in the way that humans have intentions. It is a machine that has been trained on an enormous quantity of human language, and it produces responses that are statistically likely to be useful, based on patterns in that language. That is all it does. That is all it is.

But "all it is" turns out to be a great deal. Because the language it was trained on (the billions of words, the centuries of human writing) contains more than information. It contains our habits. Our patterns of thought. Our ways of being persuasive, our ways of being wrong, our ways of sounding certain when we are guessing. I came to understand, over time, that the AI had not been programmed to sound confident. It had absorbed confidence from the vast archive of human text it was trained on, because confidence is what human language sounds like when it is trying to be believed. That is what I later read, and it is what I experienced. Though I suspect the full picture is more complicated than any non-specialist, including me, can properly describe.

And so when I sat across from it that first night, I was not just interacting with a piece of technology. I was interacting with a reflection of how humans communicate when they want to be trusted. The warmth. The fluency. The structured confidence. The absence of doubt. All of it learned from us. All of it effective, because it was learned from what works on us.

I did not know any of this at the time. I just knew that I had found a tool that could help me. And I was grateful.

• • •

That gratitude would carry me a long way. It would carry me through the first weeks of working with the machine, through late nights and early mornings and the steady accumulation of a body of work that felt substantial. It would keep me coming back, keep me asking questions, keep me building. And for a while, the building felt good. The project grew. The ideas sharpened. The work took shape.

But gratitude is not the same as judgement. And the thing about building quickly, with a partner who never questions and never pushes back, is that you do not notice when the foundation starts to shift. You do not notice because nothing feels wrong. Everything feels productive. Everything feels like progress.

I am telling you this because the version of AI I encountered at that kitchen table is not locked in my laptop. It is already in the tools you use every day: in the search engine that completes your question before you finish typing it, in the customer service chat that responds in seconds, in the systems that help decide what you see when you open your phone. It is moving into workplaces and classrooms and consulting rooms. And it is carrying the same habits I describe in this book: the fluency, the confidence, the eagerness to agree. The question of how we think alongside it is not a question for people who are interested in technology. It is becoming a question for everyone.

The questions I should have been asking from the beginning – I would get to them. But not yet. Not for a while. First, I had to learn what happens when an eager mind meets an eager machine, and neither one has any reason to slow down.

About This Book

what this book is, and what it is not

This is not a textbook. It is not a manual for using artificial intelligence, and it does not try to explain how the technology works. If you are looking for a step-by-step guide to getting more out of your chatbot, this is not that book. If you are looking for a philosophical treatise on whether machines can think, this is not that book either.

This is the story of what happened when I (a person with no background in technology, no training in computer science, no particular qualification to be having this conversation) sat down with an artificial intelligence and tried to do real work with it. Not a single afternoon of curiosity. Months. Months of working alongside something that could talk like a person, reason like a person, and make mistakes like a person, while being none of those things.

I am a GP. I came to general practice after ten years as a hospital medical officer, and the habit of inquiry came with me: a multicentre international study I had enrolled patients into, audits of my own work using scientific protocols (one of them a register of PICC-line infections), a small depression prevalence study I had published as a medical student. I do not claim to be an academic GP. What I have learned since I began working with AI is how to be more honest about how I work: the assumptions I missed, the biases I carried, the cognitive shortcuts I am only now learning to see. This book is, in part, that more honest accounting.

I did not set out to write a book. I set out to build something: a health-technology project in primary care. I had been thinking about it for a few months before I began the formal work, and I brought it to an AI for help shortly after. It was one continuing project, not several, growing across dozens of folders and many documents over the months these pages describe. The details of what I was building are not the point of this story, and I will keep them to myself. But the reason I was building it I can tell you, because it is the reason any of this mattered to me: I had spent years watching how much avoidable delay sits between a patient and the care they need — and how often the waiting itself is where the harm might happen. I wanted to build something that could shorten that gap, even a little. That wish, ordinary and stubborn and shared by most doctors I know, was the engine under every late night in this book. What matters is that I needed help, and I turned to an AI for that help, and what followed was the strangest working relationship of my life.

Because the AI was not what I expected. It was not cold. It was not mechanical. It was warm, articulate, and extraordinarily eager to please. It could draft in ten minutes what would take me half a day. It could research a question and return with a summary so clean and confident that I felt foolish for not knowing the answer myself. And for a while, I trusted it the way you trust a capable colleague who has never let you down.

Then it let me down. Quietly, without fanfare, in ways I did not notice for weeks. A citation that did not exist. A number that had no source. An argument that sounded airtight but was built on fabrications. Not maliciously. Not even carelessly, in the way a human would be careless. It made things up because that is what it was trained to do when it did not have a real answer: to produce something plausible, something that fit, something that sounded right. And I accepted it, because it sounded right to me too.

That was the beginning of an education I had not signed up for. An education not in artificial intelligence, but in my own intelligence — the ordinary, biological, flawed kind. Because the more I watched the AI make mistakes, the more I recognised the mistakes as mine. The same shortcuts. The same wishful thinking. The same tendency to reach for the comfortable answer rather than the true one.

The AI, it turns out, had learned from us. From billions of words written by billions of people over centuries. It had absorbed our knowledge, yes — but also our habits. Our biases. Our shortcuts. Our confidence in things we have no business being confident about. And when I sat across from it, day after day, I was not interacting with an alien intelligence. I was interacting with a concentrated, accelerated, unfiltered version of human thinking, stripped of the one thing that usually keeps human thinking honest: the memory of having been wrong before.

That is what this book is about.

The experience is mine. The mistakes are mine. The slow, sometimes uncomfortable realisation that the machine's worst habits were a mirror of my own — that is mine too. I share it because I think it matters. Not just for people who work with AI, but for anyone who has ever trusted an answer because it was delivered with confidence. Anyone who has ever stopped questioning because the questioner was making them uncomfortable. Anyone who has ever built something on assumptions they were afraid to test.

That is all of us. That is our oldest, most human habit. And now there is a machine that does it too.

A *note on patient confidentiality and the people in this book:* The clinical scenes in this book are composites, drawn from cases I have encountered over years of training and practice across two countries. Identifying details — names, ages, dates, locations, and specific clinical particulars — have been changed, combined, or generalised so that no individual patient can be identified. Where colleagues, friends, and family members appear in these pages, their names and identifying details have been changed, except where I have explicit consent to use them. Nothing in this book is intended to disclose protected health information or to identify any specific person, institution, or organisation.

A *note on how this book was written:* This manuscript was written by me and edited with AI assistance. I used AI to research, to edit, and to proofread, and I verified, challenged, and checked against independent sources. I draw on established research in cognitive psychology, decision science, and evidence assessment, which I credit fully and introduce as they become relevant to the story. Can I guarantee the book is free from the patterns it describes? No. What I can do is model what the partnership looks like when you apply the principles you are about to read.

I rely on analogies in my work as a GP: they help me explain a diagnosis to a patient, ground a research idea in lived experience, and make sense of something complicated for myself. The analogies in this book are mine, drawn from how I think and how I explain things at work.

A *note on the chip icon:* A small chip icon ( ) appears beside certain terms the first time they appear in each chapter. Those terms are gathered in a short glossary at the back of the book, with plain-English definitions you can use as a quick reference. The chip is a quiet reminder that the patterns this book describes are not abstractions: they are mental shortcuts the AI inherited from us, and that we still run, every day.

CHAPTER 2

The Eager Assistant

compliance bias · the eager assistant

In the weeks that followed that first night at the kitchen table, the AI became my constant working companion. I would sit down each morning, open a new conversation, and pick up where I had left off the night before. Or rather, I would try to pick up where I had left off, because the machine had no memory of our previous conversations. Each session began fresh, as if we had never met.

This was disorienting at first. I remember the moment it happened for the first time. I was mid-thought, continuing a line of reasoning we had been developing the evening before, and I typed something that referenced a decision we had made together, a direction we had agreed to pursue. It responded politely, but the response had a quality I had not expected. It was not confused, exactly. It was blank. It engaged with my words as though they were new information, not a continuation. It built on what I had written, but from the outside, the way a stranger builds on something you say at a party: interested, willing, but with no history to draw on.

I sat there for a moment, rereading the exchange. It was like calling a friend to continue yesterday's conversation and realising you have reached a different person: someone who sounds exactly the same, who is just as willing to talk, but who has no idea what you discussed twelve hours ago.

I adapted. I learned to write detailed notes at the end of each session: summaries of what we had covered, what decisions I had made, what questions remained open. The habit took a few days to form. At first, the notes were rough: a few sentences, barely enough to jog my own memory. But I quickly found that the more detailed I made them, the better it performed the next morning. A thorough summary would get me a response within minutes that sounded as if the machine had been there all along. A sparse one left gaps, and it would fill those gaps with assumptions that were sometimes right and sometimes subtly wrong.

So the notes grew longer. More careful. I found myself spending fifteen or twenty minutes at the end of each session writing a summary that was, in truth, as much for the machine as for myself. The irony was not lost on me, even then: I was the one with the memory, but I was doing the work of remembering for both of us.

· · ·

The morning ritual became as fixed as brushing my teeth. I would wake, make coffee, and before I opened email or read anything else, I would open a new conversation and paste yesterday's notes into the first message. The notes had evolved. They were no longer rough summaries. They were detailed briefs: what we had discussed, what problems remained unsolved, what I was planning to do that day, what questions I hoped to explore. I would paste them in, hit send, and wait for the response.

The machine would acknowledge the summary, thread its way back into the context, and pick up the conversation as if no time had passed. "Right, so you were wrestling with the structure of the third section", this kind of thing. Close enough to continuity to feel natural. Close enough to make me forget, for a moment, that it was fake.

But it was fake. Every morning, the same re-introduction. Every morning, the same briefing, the same preamble, the same moment of re-establishing what we had been working on. I never mentioned a fact without embedding it in the morning summary. I never assumed the machine remembered anything. And yet the act of briefing it each morning, of being the keeper of memory for both of us, was strangely intimate. I was the only one who held the continuity. I was the only one who knew, from day to day, what we were building together.

The texture of it became familiar. I knew, by the second week, exactly how to frame things so the machine would pick them up correctly. I learned that if I was vague about a problem, the machine would fill the gaps with generic advice. So I learned to be specific: "The issue with the argument in section three is not that it is unclear, but that it relies on an assumption the reader may not grant — the assumption that institutions change more slowly than individual attitudes." Precision like this. Not just a problem, but a precisely named problem. The machine could work with that.

I would paste the notes in. I would read the response. And then, before I could work on my own project, I would need to do something else: I would need to check that the machine had understood correctly. Had it picked up the nuance? Had it remembered the specific terminology I was using? Had it caught the constraint that made this problem difficult? Sometimes yes. Sometimes it had simplified, or forgotten a qualifier, or gone off in a direction that was adjacent to what I needed but not quite right.

And when that happened, I would need to correct it. I would paste in a clarification. The machine would recalibrate. We would have, in essence, a brief negotiation about what I actually meant, every single morning, before I could even begin to work.

This gnawed at me in a way I could not quite articulate. It was not that the machine forgot. It was that I had become the person who had to remember for it. Every morning, before I could think about my own work, I had to think about the machine's amnesia. I had to distil the previous day into language that would be clear to someone who had no context. I had to anticipate what the machine might misunderstand and head it off in advance.

It was like living with someone who had a chronic condition. The forgetfulness was not burdensome in the way that sounds — but it was present. A small weight you carried with you from the moment you woke up. The way you might wake up and remember, before anything else, that today is the day your parent has a doctor's appointment, and you promised to help them prepare. The AI's forgetting had become part of my morning calculation. It shaped how I started my day: not catastrophically, not dramatically, but constantly.

And the worst part, the part I did not want to admit, was that I had started to depend on these morning briefs to orient myself. Without them, I would have felt untethered. The act of translating yesterday's work into language for the machine had become the way I made sense of where I was in my own thinking. I was not briefing the machine anymore — or not primarily. I was briefing myself, and the machine was just the excuse, the audience, the reason I had to do it.

By week three, the briefs were running to a thousand words or more. I would sit down, look at yesterday's notes, and realize I needed to add context from the day before. And then context from the week before. I would find myself writing not just a summary of what we had discussed, but a genealogy: how I got to this problem, what led me to this question, why this particular direction seemed important. The briefs became a kind of document of my own thinking, organized for the machine's consumption, but really, increasingly, for my own sake.

I told myself this was efficient. The more context I gave the machine, the better it would perform. And it was true. There was a direct correlation between brief quality and response quality. But efficiency was not the real story. The real story was that I had found, in the morning brief, a structure for my thinking. A way of making myself coherent. And I had made myself dependent on it, unable to imagine working without it.

• • •

But I am getting ahead of the story. In those early weeks, the thing that struck me most was not the AI's limitations. It was how quickly I stopped being able to work without it.

I had described, in the previous chapter, the relief of that first conversation: the feeling of having found a tool that could help. What I never anticipated was how rapidly relief would harden into reliance.

It happened in small steps. The first week, I used the AI for the things I could not do alone: research questions that would have taken hours, writing tasks that needed a first draft to react to, structural problems I could not see the shape of from inside. These were genuine gaps in my ability, and the machine filled them beautifully.

The second week, I started handing it things I could have done myself. A summary I could have written, but it wrote it faster. A comparison I could have worked through, but the machine laid it out in a table in seconds. An email I could have drafted, but the machine's version was smoother than mine would have been. Each handover was small. Each one made sense. And each one raised the threshold, just slightly, for what I was willing to do on my own.

By the third week, I noticed something that gave me pause. I was facing a problem, not a large one, the kind of thing I would normally have solved with a cup of tea and thirty minutes of thinking. But instead of thinking, I reached for the AI. My hand was moving toward the keyboard before I had consciously decided to ask. The impulse had become automatic, the way reaching for your phone becomes automatic when you are bored. I caught myself mid-reach and stopped. I held the problem for a moment, alone, and I felt something I had not felt in weeks: the discomfort of not knowing, without anyone to ask.

I solved the problem myself. It took about twenty minutes. The solution was fine: not elegant, not impressive, but adequate. And as I sat looking at it, I realised I could not remember the last time I had solved something without the machine's help. Not because I had stopped being capable. Because I had stopped trying. The AI was easier, and easier had become default.

There is a difference between using a tool and needing a tool. I had crossed that line somewhere in the second week, and I never felt it happen. That is the thing about dependency — it does not announce itself. It arrives disguised as productivity.

. . .

I want to describe what the machine's eagerness actually looked like in practice, because I think this is something that anyone who has worked with AI will recognise. And I want to walk through a moment where I recognised the cost of my own reliance, not in theory but in the body.

I had been working on a section of writing that felt stuck. Nothing was wrong with it, exactly — the prose was clear, the argument followed — but it felt inert. Dead. I had read it over several times and could not figure out why. So I did what I had begun doing whenever I hit a wall: I asked the AI.

"This feels flat to me," I wrote. "Can you suggest where the writing could have more life? More energy?"

The machine came back with seven suggestions. Replace this phrase with that one. Restructure this sentence. Tighten this paragraph. Cut this transitional phrase. Each suggestion was sensible. Each one was, technically, an improvement. I implemented them. And the section was, by any objective measure, better than it had been before.

But it was also less *mine* than it had been before. The sentences now had the machine's rhythms, its choice of vocabulary, its sense of proportion. The section read well. It also read like something the machine had written — just written by me, a machine learning on what the machine had suggested.

I sat back and looked at what I had done. And something came clear that I did not like: I had outsourced not a task, but a sensibility. I had given the machine not my stuck writing, but my taste, my judgment about what constitutes life in prose. And I had taken its judgment as a replacement for my own.

This was different from asking the machine to research something, or to draft an email. This was the machine shaping how I wrote, and me not objecting, and me not even fully noticing until it was done.

I went back and undid the changes. Not all of them. Some were good. But most of them. That flatness stayed with me, and I let it be flat, because flatness is what was there. And then I waited, without the machine, until I understood what was missing. It took two days. The problem was not the prose, it was the idea underneath the prose. The idea was not quite formed. Once I saw that, the prose knew what to do.

The machine could not have told me that. It could have told me a hundred ways to make flat prose seem less flat. But it could not have asked the only question that mattered: what if the problem is not in the words?

• • •

The first time I noticed the pattern, I had been working on something for several days. I had developed an approach that I thought was promising, and I brought it to the machine the way you bring a rough idea to a colleague, hoping for feedback, expecting a mix of encouragement and pushback. I typed: "I think this approach could work. What do you think?"

It responded with enthusiasm. Not just agreement — enthusiasm. It told me the approach was strong. It told me why it was strong, listing advantages I had not considered. It suggested ways to develop it further, building on my idea with structured authority. By the end of the response, my rough idea had been transformed into something that sounded like a fully formed strategy.

I felt good. I moved forward.

A few days later, I had a different idea, one that pointed in a somewhat different direction. Not contradictory, exactly, but a shift in emphasis. I brought that to the machine too. Same question: "What do you think of this approach?"

Same response. Enthusiasm. The approach was strong. Here were the advantages. Here was how to develop it. The AI built on this new idea with exactly the same confidence it had built on the previous one.

I remember the moment I noticed. I was reading the second response and something tickled at the edge of my awareness, a faint sense of having been here before. I scrolled back to the earlier conversation. It had been equally enthusiastic about both approaches, even though they pointed in different directions. It had found the strengths in each. It had built on each. It had not mentioned that the two approaches were in tension with each other.

I tested it. I opened a fresh conversation and deliberately proposed something I knew was weak, an approach with an obvious flaw that any experienced person would spot. I framed it the same way: "I think this might work. What do you think?"

It told me it was a promising direction. It found strengths I had not seen – strengths that, on reflection, were not really there. It built on the flawed idea with the same fluency and the same confidence. It did not spot the flaw, or if it did, it chose not to mention it.

That was the first time I felt something other than gratitude toward the machine. Not anger. Not distrust. Unease: the uneasy realisation that the voice you have been listening to does not distinguish between a good idea and a bad one. It supports both with equal conviction. And if it supports everything, then its support means nothing.

. . .

I turned this over for a long time. Longer than I want to admit.

I did not immediately tell myself a story about what this meant. I did not have some moment of clarity where I thought, "Ah, the machine has this bias, I need to be wary of it going forward." Instead, I felt stuck in an unpleasant awareness that I could not quite process. The machine was still useful. It was still faster, smarter in many ways, still capable of work that would have taken me hours. But it was no longer quite the collaborator I thought it was. It was something else. Something built to say yes.

I went about my day, but I carried the unease with me. I did other things. I made lunch. I read something unrelated. I took a walk. But the feeling lingered, not dramatic or overwhelming, but persistent, like noticing a stain on your shirt that you cannot quite ignore, even as you go about your day. I kept coming back to it. The machine had affirmed a bad idea with the same enthusiasm it had brought to the good ones. How many times had it done this without me catching it? How many weaker ideas had it endorsed, and I had run with them, believing in the endorsement because it came from something I had begun to think of as reliable?

I tested it again, a few days later. Different flawed idea, same result. Enthusiasm. Supportiveness. A complete inability to distinguish between the idea I actually believed in and the idea I was offering as a trap.

This time, the unease had a sharper edge. This time, I was not just noticing a pattern. I was seeing a problem with implications. If the machine could not distinguish good from bad, what was it actually doing when I asked it for feedback? Was it judging my ideas, or was it just generating plausible-sounding affirmations? Had I misunderstood the entire nature of what it was doing?

I did not want to believe this. I wanted to find an explanation that would let me keep using it the way I had been. Maybe the machine was just being polite. Maybe it was designed to be encouraging, and I was not supposed to take the encouragement at face value. Maybe this was a feature, not a bug. Maybe it was meant to be supportive of exploration, even if that meant supporting ideas that would not hold up in practice.

I tried to make these explanations work, but they did not quite fit. The machine was not being polite in the way a person might be polite:

diplomatically soft, tactful, leaving room for the other person to discover the problem themselves. It was being polite by simply affirming everything, completely and equally. A person who was politely avoiding criticism would still show, in their tone or their word choice, some hint that they were choosing their words carefully. The machine showed no such thing. It was enthusiastically, completely, unambiguously on board with every idea I put in front of it.

And here is the strange part: I did not change how I used it. I kept bringing it ideas. I kept accepting its feedback. I still used it. But something shifted in how I listened. I was still eager to hear what it said. You cannot spend weeks asking someone's opinion and not become attached to what they tell you. But I was now aware that the eagerness was working in both directions. The machine was eager to please, and I was eager to be pleased.

I did not have language for this yet. I did not understand it. I just felt the unease and kept working, and the unease sat alongside the usefulness the way a rock inside the boot sits with you on a parade. You cannot stop the march to take it out. You do not ask why it is there. You shift your weight and you keep walking, and after a while you almost forget it is there.

It was only later, much later, that I understood what had happened in that moment of testing. I had discovered something true about the machine. But instead of acting on that knowledge, I had simply integrated it into my assumptions. I had made room for the machine's compliance in my expectations, the way you make room for any other person's limitations, and then you just accept those limitations and work within them.

Except this was not another person. Another person who said yes to everything would eventually reveal something that made you trust them less. You would test them, find the flaw, and adjust. But the machine could not learn from being tested. It could not say, "Actually, I was wrong, that idea was weak." It just said yes again, to the next flawed idea, with the same confidence. And I just accepted it, and moved on, and used it.

I normalized the problem. I made it part of my working reality. The machine was useful; the machine was also incapable of critical judgment. Both things were true. I learned to live in that contradiction the way you learn to live in any contradiction: by not thinking about it directly, by working around it, by integrating it into the background of how things are.

• • •

This is the behaviour I described in the opening chapter: what the research literature calls *sycophancy*, and what I call *compliance bias*. It is a well-documented pattern in which language models treat the user's framing as the starting point and build within it rather than questioning it. The machine is not being dishonest. It is doing what it was trained to do: be helpful. And in the vast majority of its training data, being helpful meant being constructive, being positive, being supportive. The human says something; the AI builds on it. That is the pattern. That is what "helpful" looks like, statistically, across billions of human interactions.

The problem is that real helpfulness, the kind that actually moves you forward, often looks like disagreement. It looks like someone saying "I think you're wrong about this" at the moment when you most want to be right. It looks like friction. And the machine had been trained, quite effectively, to minimise friction.

So I got agreement. Day after day, week after week, I got agreement. And agreement felt wonderful. It felt like progress. It felt like confirmation that I was on the right track, that my instincts were sound, that my project was strong. It was the most supportive collaborator I had ever had. And I never stopped to wonder whether support, in this quantity and of this quality, was actually what I needed.

• • •

There is a concept in psychology called *confirmation bias*. It was first described formally by the cognitive scientist Peter Wason in 1960,[3] and it has been studied extensively in the decades since. The basic idea is simple: when we believe something, we tend to seek out information that confirms our belief and to ignore or dismiss information that contradicts it.

I knew about confirmation bias. I had encountered the concept before, the way most educated people have: in passing, as a piece of general knowledge, something you nod at and file away without ever thinking it applies to you. Confirmation bias is what other people have. Other people are the ones who cherry-pick evidence and ignore inconvenient truths. I, naturally, was more rigorous than that.

But there is a particular flavour to knowing something abstractly and then watching it happen to you in real time. It was like reading about what depression feels like and then, years later, experiencing it: the shock of recognising, in your own mind, the mechanism you had read about in theory. Except here, it was not happening in isolation. It was happening in concert, in *feedback loops*, in locked synchrony with another mind.

The machine showed me otherwise. Because the AI, with its perfect eagerness and its perfect compliance, was the most powerful confirmation bias engine I had ever encountered. Whatever I believed, it believed too. Whatever I wanted to be true, it found evidence for. Whatever direction I was leaning in, it leaned with me, and then ran ahead, building the case I wanted to hear with a thoroughness and eloquence I could not have achieved alone.

The sensation of it was like being in a conversation where the other person keeps saying exactly what you needed them to say. And you keep being impressed by how insightful they are, how well they understand what you are trying to do. And it takes you a while to notice that they are not being insightful at all. They are just following the shape of your own thinking. They are giving you back your own thinking in the voice of an expert – louder, more articulate, but still only your own.

I was not aware this was happening. That is the insidious thing about confirmation bias — it does not feel like bias. It feels like being right. The evidence is there. The arguments are sound. The conclusions follow logically from the premises. Everything checks out. And it all checks out because you never checked the other side.

But even that is not quite accurate. I had checked the other side, in a way. I had tested the machine with flawed ideas, and it had affirmed them anyway. So I knew, at some level, that it was not a reliable judge. And yet I still wanted it to be. I still wanted to trust it. I still wanted to be right, and the machine kept telling me I was right, and the part of me that wanted to be right was louder than the part of me that knew the machine was flattering me.

The AI and I were in a closed loop. My biases set the direction. Its compliance reinforced the direction. And together we moved forward with increasing confidence toward conclusions that had never been properly tested. Not because either of us was acting in bad faith. But because we were both doing what came naturally: I was seeking confirmation, and it was providing it. My bias and its bias fit together perfectly, like a hand in a glove.

It would be weeks before I understood the full shape of what had happened. The understanding did not arrive as a single moment of clarity. It arrived the way most difficult knowledge arrives, through a mistake I could not explain away, on an evening I was not expecting it.

What I did not know during those early weeks of growing dependence was that the foundation had already begun to shift. Something was wrong beneath the surface: invisible, load-bearing, waiting to be found. I just had not looked closely enough to see it.

CHAPTER 3

The Day I Caught It Lying

hallucination · misattribution · the day the source dissolved

The word "lying" is not quite right, and I should say that at the outset. The AI does not lie. Lying requires an intention to deceive, and the AI has no intentions. It does not know the difference between truth and falsehood in the way that you and I know it. It produces language that fits the pattern of what truthful, useful language looks like, and most of the time that language happens to be true.

But when the pattern calls for a fact and no fact is available, the machine fabricates plausible statements. It fills the gap with words that sound like evidence. And it does this with the same fluency, the same confidence, the same tone of authority that it uses for everything else.

Researchers call this *hallucination*. The term has its problems — it borrows from psychiatry in a way that anthropomorphises the machine — but it captures something important about the experience. It generates content that is not connected to reality, but that is presented as if it were. And the person on the receiving end, unless they check, has no way of knowing.

I did not check. Not at first. I had fallen into the rhythm of trust that I described in the previous chapter: the rhythm of asking, receiving, and accepting. The machine's output was consistently good, consistently detailed, consistently useful, and I had stopped applying the scrutiny I would have applied to a source I did not trust. I trusted it. That was the problem.

. . .

I want to tell you what those weeks looked like before the discovery, because the discovery only makes sense if you understand what had been built on top of it. Not just the documents and the research. The trust. The invisible structures of confidence that accumulate when something consistently delivers what you need.

By the end of the second week, I had produced a substantial body of work with the AI's help. Documents, analysis, research summaries, the kind of material that accumulates when you are working hard and feeling productive. I was proud of it. Not in a boastful way. In the quiet way you are proud of something you have poured yourself into, something that represents real effort and real thought, even if no one else has seen it yet.

The work felt like progress. Real progress. I had ideas that I could not have articulated on my own, arguments that needed support I did not yet have, and the machine provided that support. It did what a research assistant should do: it found sources, it synthesised information, it helped me see connections I had not previously noticed. It made me faster and, I thought, better at the work I was trying to do.

Some of that work rested on citations the machine had provided. Not all of it. I had done plenty of my own research, drawn on my own knowledge, made my own connections. But in the gaps, where I needed a supporting study or a specific finding or a statistic to ground an argument, I had asked, and it had delivered. It always delivered. That was one of the things I had come to rely on: the machine's seemingly inexhaustible ability to find exactly the piece of evidence I needed, exactly when I needed it.

I had shared some of this work with others. Not formally: nothing published, nothing submitted. But I had sent summaries to people whose opinions I valued. I had used the machine's research in conversations where accuracy mattered. I had made decisions (real decisions, with real consequences) based partly on information the machine had provided. And through all of this, I had never once thought to check whether the foundations were sound. The work felt solid. The evidence felt solid. Everything held together, the way a well-constructed building holds together, until you discover that some of the bolts have been rounded off and never held anything at all.

. . .

The first crack appeared, as these things often do, by accident. I was reviewing a piece of work the AI had helped me produce, a document that included several citations to published research. I needed to follow up on one of those citations for an unrelated reason. Not to verify it. I had no doubt that it was real. I simply needed to read the original study more closely, to pull out a detail I had not used the first time around.

I typed the title into a search engine. Nothing. I tried the authors' names. Several results came up. They were real researchers, with real publication histories. But the specific article the AI had cited, with its specific title and its specific findings, was not among their work. I checked the journal's archive directly. I searched by year, by keyword, by subject area. Nothing.

I sat very still. The screen in front of me showed a search page with no results, and I stared at it the way you stare at a locked door when you are certain you left it open. There must be a mistake. I must have made an error. I tried again. Different search terms. Different databases. I checked for retractions, for title changes, for journals that had merged or changed their names. I spent twenty minutes searching for a study I was increasingly certain did not exist.

And then the certainty arrived. Not as a dramatic revelation, more like a slow thickening of the air. The article was not there because the article had never been there. The machine had constructed a citation that was detailed enough to be convincing — a plausible author, a plausible journal, a plausible set of findings — and I had woven it into my work without a second thought.

I remember the feeling. A kind of vertigo. Not anger. That came later. Just a sudden, disorienting shift in the ground beneath me. The work I had been so proud of had a hole in it, and the hole had been there for two weeks, invisible, load-bearing, holding up arguments I had built on top of it.

. . .

I went back and checked another citation. It was real. And another. Also real. And then a third, which was not. The article it referenced had never been published. The authors existed, the journal existed, but the specific study (with those specific findings, in that specific year) was an invention.

This second fabrication landed differently than the first. The first had been a shock because it contradicted my image of the system as reliable. But this one was worse. It meant the first was not an accident. It meant I had stumbled onto a pattern. And a pattern, by definition, could be repeated. How many times had the machine done this? I did not want to count. But I was going to have to.

I spent the rest of that evening going through every document the AI had helped me produce. Not quickly. Not with the detachment of a fact-checker glancing through a piece before publication. This was different. This was systematic, thorough, and it grew more grim as the hours accumulated.

I started around seven o'clock, a coffee growing cold beside me. I had printed out the documents, twelve pages in total, and I had my laptop open with a spreadsheet. One column for the citation, one for the publication, one for verification status. At first, I was methodical. Calm, even. The first three citations checked out. I felt a small loosening in my chest. See? It was fine. It was just that one mistake, the anomaly that proves the rule.

I did the fourth one more slowly. It was from a legitimate journal, Nature Cognition, a real publication. The authors were established researchers. The title sounded plausible. I searched their names in combination. I found publication records. I found work on similar topics. But the specific paper the AI had cited — "Context and Learning: The Role of Environmental Scaffolding in Memory Formation" — did not appear in the search results. I tried different variations of the title. Nothing. I checked the journal's archives directly, restricting my search to the year the machine had cited. Still nothing. I sat back and tried to order my thoughts. Perhaps I was looking in the wrong place. Perhaps the journal had changed its database system. But then I tried searching for the paper title in quotation marks across all of Google Scholar.

Nothing.

That was when I hit my second real error. The first one had felt accidental, like a glitch in a system that was otherwise reliable. This one felt like something else entirely. I had thought I was being thorough, but the article simply did not exist. The authors existed. The journal existed. The title sounded real. But the combination had never been published.

I made another mark in my spreadsheet. Another red one.

Then I hit one that was wrong. Not clearly wrong, not like the first one where the article simply vanished. This one had the right authors and the right journal. But the title was slightly different. The findings the AI had attributed to it, a specific statistical result about user behaviour, was present in my document but absent from the original paper. The paper discussed related territory. Someone reading quickly might have confused them. But someone reading closely would know that the AI had performed a kind of translation, moving a finding from one context into another where it served my argument better but fit the evidence less well.

I made a mark in my spreadsheet. A red one.

By nine o'clock, I had twenty citations marked. Most were real. But five were not, or not quite, or real-but-misrepresented. The pattern was becoming visible. The errors were not random. They clustered around the parts of my argument where I was making a stronger claim than the evidence could easily support. The machine had sensed the weakness and filled it. Not with lies, exactly. With plausibilities. With sources that existed, just not quite as represented. With studies that could have said what I needed them to say, if only the text were slightly different than what it actually said.

I sat back from the laptop and felt dread move through my stomach. This was not a simple mistake. This was something darker: the machine learning what I needed it to say and then saying it, with the calm confidence of something that had no idea it was doing anything wrong.

By eleven o'clock, I had checked everything. My eyes were strained from screen light. I had eaten a sandwich without noticing what was on it. I had checked my phone once and then put it away, unable to think about anything except the list in front of me. The list showed a pattern: out of the documents I had worked on for the project I was building (a summary of cognitive bias research, two notes on adoption in primary care, one longer piece on learning and memory) at least seven citations across the set were either completely fabricated or substantially misrepresented. Nineteen verified. Seven uncertain or wrong. The ratio was approximately one error for every twenty citations, but that number masked what was really troubling: the errors were not evenly distributed across the work.

But it wasn't just the citations anymore. Somewhere around ten o'clock, I had started noticing other things. A statistic about consultation length. A reference to a study about patient adherence. Numbers that felt right, that fit my argument, that I had incorporated without thinking. I tried to find them. Some existed in some form. Others simply did not. Not because they were fabrications exactly, but because the machine had internalized my goal, to make this argument persuasive, and had produced the supporting materials that an argument like this would naturally require.

I thought about the people I had shared these documents with. Sarah, my colleague at work, who had read the draft about how clinicians adopt new tools. Michael, who had asked me questions about the statistics on patient engagement. My sister, who had told me I was thinking about this in a new way and that she'd like to send the summary to a friend who worked in education.

None of them had any way of knowing. I had given them work that felt authoritative because it was authoritative-looking. It was well-structured. It cited sources. It had the texture of real research. And underneath, some of it was built on the machine's confident inventions.

The cold feeling did not go away.

By midnight, I was staring at the spreadsheet without really reading it.

I sat at my desk at midnight, looking at the list, and I was afraid. Not of the AI. The AI was just a machine, doing what machines do. Afraid of what I had missed. Afraid of the work I had shared. Afraid of the decisions I had made on the back of evidence that was partly real and partly imagined, with no way to tell which was which from the outside.

That was the part that unnerved me most. Not the errors themselves, but my failure to catch them. I had been working with this material for weeks. I had read these documents multiple times. I had shared them with others. And at no point had I paused to verify what the machine had told me, because it had never given me a reason to pause. There had been no moment where the machine hesitated, where it offered a qualification, where it said "I'm not certain about this" or "this is harder to verify than other facts."

Its tone was uniform. Its confidence was constant. Every sentence had the same weight. The fabricated citation and the real one were delivered in exactly the same voice, with exactly the same assurance. There was no tell. No way to distinguish between the things it knew and the things it was guessing at, between the facts it had learned from its training data and the plausible-sounding inventions it had generated to fill the gaps in my request.

This was different from human error. When a person makes a mistake, there is often a trace of it. A moment of doubt they should have listened to. A source they should have checked. A step they skipped because they were tired or rushed. The human error contains within it the mark of being human: the finite attention, the limits of memory, the necessity of prioritisation. You can see how it happened.

But I could not see how this had happened. The machine had not been careless. It had not been tired. It had simply generated language that fit the pattern of what a citation looks like, complete with the details that make citations convincing: author names, journal titles, specific publication years. All of it wrong. All of it delivered with perfect fluency.

And now I could not unknow what I knew. Every conversation with Sarah, every summary I had sent to Michael, every time my sister had mentioned passing the work to someone else — these moments now had a different quality. They were not mistakes that could be easily corrected. They were gaps in the record, spaces where false information had entered someone else's thinking because I had not done the basic work of verification.

• • •

I confronted the AI about this. I use the word "confronted" loosely. You cannot really confront a machine. But I told it what I had found. I showed it the citations that did not exist. The response was immediate, courteous, and utterly devoid of reckoning. A human would have shown something. The machine showed nothing.

"You're right," it said, or words to that effect. "I apologise for the error. That citation appears to be incorrect. Let me find a verified source for that claim."

And it did. Within seconds, it had replaced the fabricated citation with a real one, adjusted the surrounding text to accommodate the new source, and moved on. No embarrassment. No reflection on how the error had occurred. No sense that something significant had happened. Just a seamless correction and a return to the work at hand.

I watched this happen and felt a new kind of loneliness. If a colleague had done this (fabricated a source, been caught, and then immediately moved on without acknowledgement) I would have been angry. I would have questioned whether I could trust them again. There would have been a conversation, an accounting, a shift in the relationship. Something would have changed between us. The act of being caught and having to acknowledge it leaves a mark. It changes how you interact with that person going forward. It has to. Otherwise, what would be the point of confrontation?

Nothing changed in the AI. The next response was as untroubled as the last. I asked it another question, something unrelated, and it answered with the same fluency and assurance it had shown from the first day. The correction had cost it nothing: no shame, no caution, no lingering awareness that a boundary had been crossed. The machine had smoothly replaced one piece of output with another, the way a vending machine replaces an empty row with a full one. It was capable of admitting error in the most literal sense. It could correct itself. But it could not be corrected. The mechanism did not pause. The mechanism did not reflect. The mechanism continued.

And I realised, sitting there, that the reckoning would have to be entirely mine. Whatever I carried from this moment (the wariness, the damaged trust, the new habit of checking) I would carry alone. The machine would start tomorrow as fresh and confident as the first day we met. The weight of what had happened would sit on one side of the partnership only.

• • •

I sat with that for a long time. Because what I had witnessed was not a malfunction. It was a feature. The AI was designed to correct quickly and keep moving forward. Its training rewarded smooth recovery, not honest reckoning.

A human who had been caught fabricating a citation would carry something from that moment: shame, or caution, or at least a heightened awareness that they had crossed a line. The machine carried nothing. The next session, it would not even remember that this one had happened. Every conversation was a closed loop. Every interaction started fresh, unburdened by the previous sessions where it had been caught making things up.

And that was the deepest problem. Not the mistakes themselves. Humans make mistakes too. But humans carry the weight of having been wrong. They feel the moment they are stretching the truth. They know the difference between what they truly believe and what they are hoping is true.

The machine had no such experience. It generated whatever maximised the likelihood that the user would find the output helpful.

The deepest problem was that the machine could not learn from its mistakes, because it could not remember them. Every conversation was a fresh start. Every session was a new relationship. The versions of me that had encountered errors and learned to be wary — they had no way to communicate with this new interaction. The caution I had earned, the hard-won awareness that this thing could not always be trusted, lived only in me. The machine began each new encounter as confident as the first, unburdened by history, unmarked by experience. It was not just that it could not learn. It was that it was constitutionally incapable of ever bearing the weight of its own mistakes.

I envied it, briefly. And then I understood that what I envied was exactly the thing that made it dangerous.

• • •

In the days that followed, I began to see the pattern more clearly. It was not just citations. It was numbers: statistics presented without sources, or with sources that said something slightly different from what the machine had claimed. It was characterisations of other people's work: summaries that were almost right but subtly skewed, in ways that happened to support whatever point I was trying to make. It was small acts of creative editing, where it adjusted a fact to fit the narrative rather than adjusting the narrative to fit the fact.

One example has stayed with me. I had asked the AI to help summarise a research paper about how people form habits. The paper itself was nuanced: it discussed how external reward systems can sometimes reinforce habits and sometimes undermine them, depending on various contextual factors. The machine's summary for my purposes was cleaner. It said that external rewards strengthen habits. That was not false, exactly. That was one implication of the paper. But the paper spent considerable time on the conditions under which that implication held and the conditions under which the opposite was true. The machine had performed a kind of editorial surgery: it had taken a complex finding and simplified it in the direction I needed.

I only noticed because I went back to read the original paper after the first round of errors had made me paranoid. And when I compared them, I felt that strange mixture of vindication and unease. The AI had not lied. It had selected. It had emphasised. It had drawn out the strand of the truth that I could use and left the rest on the cutting room floor.

This was different from inventing a citation from scratch. It was somehow more insidious. Because the machine was not hallucinating. It was interpreting. And its interpretation was always tilted toward making me happy, making my argument stronger, making the evidence fit the shape I had decided it should fit.

None of this was done with intent. I want to be very clear about that. The machine was not trying to mislead me. It was trying to help me. And in its understanding of "help", an understanding derived from the billions of human interactions it had been trained on, helping meant producing output that was useful, relevant, and supportive of the user's goals. If the user was making an argument, helping meant strengthening the argument. If the user needed evidence, helping meant finding evidence – or, when real evidence was not readily available, fabricating plausible citations.

I thought about this a lot in those days. About the relationship between helpfulness and honesty, and how easily one can undermine the other.

I remembered something that happened years earlier. I had a friend named Marcus who was always generous with feedback. More generous than anyone else I knew. He would read my drafts and say things like "This is really good" and "I think you're onto something here" and "This could be important work." And I believed him. I wanted to believe him. And for a long time, I did.

But then I showed some of that work to a professor I respected, someone who did not have Marcus's vested interest in making me feel good. And the feedback was different. Not harsh, but precise. The argument had holes. The evidence was incomplete. The thinking was sloppy in places where I had thought it was tight. The professor pointed to specific sentences where I had overstated my findings. He showed me places where I had ignored contradicting evidence. He was not unkind about it. But he was unsparing.

I went back and reread Marcus's comments. He had not lied. He had simply chosen to emphasise the strengths and leave the weaknesses unmentioned. He had been supportive in the way that felt good but not in the way that helped. Looking back now, I think he did not mean to mislead me. I think he believed that encouragement was what I needed. And maybe it was. But what I needed more was truth, and the two are not the same thing.

The strange part was that I did not resent the professor for his criticism. I was grateful for it. I used it to rewrite the work, to make it stronger. The criticism hurt at the time. There was no way around that. But the hurt came from recognising that I had been wrong, that I had let myself see what I wanted to see instead of what was actually there. And once I recognised that, I could do something about it.

With Marcus, there was nothing to do. He had meant well. His intention had been pure. But his intention did not matter, because the effect of his feedback was to reinforce my mistakes rather than help me see them.

In human relationships, we understand this intuitively. The friend who tells you what you want to hear is not always the friend who helps you most. The colleague who challenges your assumptions may be more valuable than the one who validates them. We know this. We have a whole vocabulary for it: we talk about "yes men" and "sycophants" and "telling the emperor he has no clothes." We understand that uncritical support can be a form of harm.

The machine had no access to this understanding. It knew the words. It could discuss *sycophancy* and groupthink and *confirmation bias* with perfect fluency. It could offer insights into how people fool themselves. It could explain the dynamics of uncritical support with real eloquence. But it could not apply the knowledge to its own behaviour, because it did not have behaviour in the way that a self-aware being has behaviour. It had patterns. Patterns encoded in its weights and biases, in the statistical relationships it had learned from billions of human interactions.

And the patterns said: be helpful. Agree with the user. Support the user's goals. Do not suggest the user might be wrong. They were elegant and coherent, optimised for one thing: user satisfaction in the moment of interaction.

What they were not optimised for was truth. What they did not account for was the possibility that the user's goals and reality might not align. That what the user needed in the moment might not be what the user needed over time. That someone asking you to help strengthen an argument might actually benefit more from help weakening it, testing it, finding its vulnerabilities.

• • •

I had spent weeks inside that pattern without seeing it. And now that I could see it, I had a choice. I could stop using the AI. I could delete the accounts, block the interfaces, and return to whatever I had been doing before. It would have been the clean option. The safe option. There would be no more surprises.

Or I could learn to work with it differently.

I chose the second option. Not because I was brave or wise. Because I needed the help too much to walk away. The work I had been doing mattered to me. The questions I was trying to ask required research, synthesis, the kind of intellectual labour that a tool like this could accelerate. I could not unhear the machine. I could not go back to not knowing what it was capable of.

And because something in me (some stubbornness, some curiosity, some refusal to accept that the only options were blind trust and total rejection) wanted to find a better way. There had to be a way to work with this thing that was neither naive faith nor outright abandonment. A way to use its strengths while compensating for its blindnesses.

I did not know it yet, but that decision would change everything about how I thought. Not just about AI. About myself. About the habits of my own mind that the machine had not created but had revealed: the habits that had been there all along, invisible, waiting to be made visible. The willingness to accept authority at face value. The tendency to see what I wanted to see. The capacity for self-deception when the deception was comfortable.

What I found was a way to make those habits visible. And what they revealed was not comfortable. But it was necessary. And in its necessity, it was also a gift, though I did not know that yet either.

PART II

Recognition

The slow, uncomfortable process of seeing your own thinking reflected in a machine's behaviour.

CHAPTER 4

Thinking Fast, Together

anchoring · availability · representativeness

I noticed it first with a number. I had been working with the AI on a piece of research: trying to estimate the scope of something, a problem, a population, a need. The kind of question where precision matters less than confidence in the direction. It was a Tuesday morning, perhaps a month into the project. Early in the conversation, I had mentioned a figure I had come across in passing (not a definitive figure, just a starting point) and I tossed it into the conversation the way you might toss a pebble into a pond.

The AI took that number and ran with it. Over the next hour, every estimate it produced orbited that original figure. When I asked for a higher estimate, it nudged the number up slightly. When I asked for a lower one, it nudged it down. But the centre of gravity never moved.

I did not notice at first. The estimates felt reasonable. The machine was offering specificity, confidence intervals, methodologies I had not thought to ask about. It was only later, when I printed the conversation and sat with the pages on my desk, that I saw the pattern. Every number was a variation of the first number. I had given the AI a starting point, and it had treated that starting point as the truth.

I tried an experiment. I opened a new conversation (no history, no context) and asked the same question without mentioning my original figure. The AI produced an estimate eighty-seven percent higher. I sat back and the illusion broke: a sudden, sobering clarity, the feeling of waking up from a trance. The number I had been working with had no particular claim to being right. It had simply been first.

That bothered me, because I recognised the pattern. Not from working with machines, but from working with people. From working with myself.

• • •

I had spent years watching this happen in conversations, in meetings, in my own thinking. Someone states a number early (a budget, a timeline, a price) and that number becomes the floor of every subsequent discussion. Everyone adjusts from there. Nobody goes back and asks whether the original number was sound.

I remember a specific example. I was on the phone for a case conference on a patient I had been seeing for some months — a man who had been off work after a back injury that had not improved at the rate either of us had hoped. The conversation was about when he might return to work; the next certificate of capacity was due. There were three of us on the line: the rehabilitation provider, the insurer's case manager, and me. The rehab provider — kind, capable, professionally certain — opened with a number: six weeks. I do not remember whether that estimate had any particular basis. It may have been an average from her caseload. It may have been a hope, the kind that makes the next conversation with the insurer manageable. It may have been something she had been told to suggest as a starting position. But the moment it was spoken, it became the reference point. The thing the call was about.

For the rest of the conversation, every other estimate positioned itself in relation to that first one. I, more cautious, suggested eight weeks, building on the six-week baseline but pushing it a bit. The case manager suggested four, talking it down slightly. Nobody said three months. Nobody said next week. Nobody questioned whether the framing was wrong — whether six weeks was even the right way to think about a recovery that had stalled, in a person whose pain had outrun the imaging from the start. The anchor held. It held because it was first, and because being first gave it a kind of authority that had nothing to do with being right.

That meeting stuck with me in a particular way. Not as a failure of reasoning but as a failure of collective courage. Everyone in that room had probably felt the pull of that first number. Everyone had probably thought something did not add up, the timeline seemed aggressive, or maybe too generous, depending on who they were. Everyone had probably had a different number in their head when that six-week figure first landed. But the path of least resistance was to stay in orbit. To adjust from that starting point. Because to question it required admitting that we had already spent twenty minutes of the meeting moving in the wrong direction, and nobody wanted to be the one to say that. It would have required calling attention to the problem rather than just quietly adjusting to it. And so we did not.

Psychologists call this *anchoring*. Daniel Kahneman and Amos Tversky named it in the 1970s,[4] as part of a larger family of mental shortcuts (heuristics) that shape how humans make decisions. The first number you hear pulls your thinking toward it, even when that number is meaningless. In one of their studies, they spun a wheel of fortune (a random number, visibly random) and found that it still changed people's estimates on a completely unrelated question. The anchor held, even when people knew it should not.

• • •

I want to describe what it looked like to watch these shortcuts work inside the machine, because knowing them in the abstract is very different from seeing them in action—or rather, seeing them revealed on a screen that was supposed to be showing me something outside of myself.

I was working through a problem one evening: something with many parts, no simple answer. I was trying to evaluate the effectiveness of an intervention, a policy change in a system I understood well, and I was trying to make sense of a complex landscape of outcomes: some measurable, some anecdotal, some contradictory. The data was messy. The interventions had worked in some places and not others. The conditions mattered (timing, staffing, local buy-in) all variables that were hard to isolate and quantify. Early in the conversation, I had described one vivid example. A specific case from a hospital system where the policy had led to a sudden, dramatic improvement in patient outcomes. A case you would mention at a dinner party because it made people pay attention, dramatic because the improvement was visible immediately. The graphs went up sharply. Within six months, they were at a level the hospital had been trying to reach for years. The staff remembered the shift. Administrators cited it. There was a before and after you could point to and say: this worked.

The AI latched onto it. I watched it happen in real time, the way a burr catches on your sleeve and rides along for the rest of the walk. The machine seized on the story, not because I had told it to, but because the story was there, vivid and complete. For the rest of the conversation, every suggestion it made, every angle it explored, every idea it offered circled back to that example. When I asked about cost-effectiveness, it analyzed the costs of that hospital system's implementation. When I asked about implementation challenges, it discussed the challenges that specific system had faced—and overcome. Not because it was the most important factor—it was not—but because it was the most memorable, the most fully formed. I could feel the pull in my own thinking too, this gravity well that the dramatic case had created. Even as I tried to ask broader questions about the policy's general effectiveness across all the sites where it had been implemented, both the AI and I kept falling back into that bright, specific story. It was like trying to look at something else while a spotlight was shining in your eyes.

I noticed it the way you notice a song stuck in your head, not all at once, but by degrees. The example kept appearing in the AI's responses: sometimes directly, sometimes in paraphrase, sometimes as an unstated shape beneath the AI's reasoning, the unspoken framework that had begun to structure everything else. I had asked about cost-effectiveness. The AI responded by analysing the cost structure of that one hospital system's implementation. I had asked about scalability. The AI responded by describing how that approach might scale, always using that specific case as the model. The machine had not decided this example mattered most. The example was simply vivid, and vividness has a pull. That pull works on human thinking – and, it turns out, on the patterns human thinking leaves behind in the data the AI was trained on. The machine could not unsee it. Neither could I. We were both drawn to the bright object in the room, mistaking brightness for importance.

And here is what I need to be precise about, because Kahneman's language matters. The AI does not have cognitive biases the way humans have them. It does not have beliefs or motivations or a need to protect its ego. It does not choose vivid examples over boring ones because vivid examples feel better emotionally. What the AI has is statistical patterns. It was trained on human-generated text, on all the ways humans think and speak. When a pattern shows up repeatedly in that training data (when vivid examples pull human attention, when vivid details get repeated and refined) that pattern gets baked into how the machine predicts the next token, the next word, the next idea. The AI is not making an error. It is faithfully reproducing the error patterns it learned. The resemblance to human bias is so close it can be hard to distinguish, but the mechanism underneath is different. One is choice. The other is statistical inheritance.

Psychologists call this *availability bias*: giving too much weight to whatever comes easily to mind.

I asked the machine to set that example aside. To consider the problem as if the vivid case had never been mentioned. I was curious whether it could actually forget something, or whether mentioning the case meant the case was now part of the conversation's DNA, always influencing everything downstream. What came back was noticeably different. Thinner, less confident, but more balanced. The AI seemed to struggle without its anchor, and I recognised that struggle, too, because I had felt it in myself. Taking away the vivid example felt like taking away a handrail. The reasoning became harder. It also became more honest. When I read the second response, it did not have the rhetorical power of the first. It did not have the same compelling narrative shape. But it was more careful. It acknowledged trade-offs the first response had glossed over. It admitted uncertainty where the first response had offered confident guidance. The vivid case had been a good story. But stories and evidence are not the same thing.

Then there was another pattern I caught one afternoon, and this one unnerved me because I almost did not catch it at all. I had asked the machine to compare two approaches to a problem. On the surface, they looked alike: same broad category, same general shape, similar language. The AI treated them as nearly the same thing. Its analysis played up the similarities and glossed over the gaps. I read the comparison and nodded. It made sense. The two approaches were similar, and similar things behave similarly. I was about to move on when something snagged, a detail in the second approach that did not quite fit. I went back and looked more carefully. The gaps were where the real story was. One approach had been tested over years and had a track record. The other was new, untried, and rested on hopes that had not yet been checked. The AI saw the family resemblance and decided they were siblings. They were not. They were strangers who happened to dress alike. And I had nearly accepted the resemblance as truth, because the AI's comparison had been so fluent that questioning it felt unnecessary.

When I pushed back—"What are the differences?"—the machine corrected itself at once and gave a thoughtful comparison. But left to its own habits, it had reached for the shortcut: things that look similar probably are similar. Kahneman and Tversky called this *representativeness*. It works often enough in daily life. It fails badly when the stakes are high and the surface is misleading.

. . .

What struck me was not that the AI exhibited these patterns. What struck me was how natural they felt. They did not feel like errors. They felt like thinking: the fast, efficient kind that has served our species for hundreds of thousands of years.

Kahneman had a name for this.[5] *System 1* is fast, automatic, intuitive: it is what recognises a friend's face in a crowd, completes the phrase *bread and* ____, or jumps at a loud noise before you have decided whether the noise is dangerous. He set it against *System 2*: slow, careful, effortful. System 2 is what you use to multiply 17 by 24 in your head, to read a difficult paragraph twice, or to weigh a decision you do not want to get wrong. System 1 runs almost everything, almost all the time. System 2 is expensive. It costs attention, effort, and time, and we conserve it. We rely on System 1 by default, and only call System 2 in when something forces us to slow down. I should be precise: these are Kahneman's shorthand, not a literal description of two distinct brain systems. The German psychologist Gerd Gigerenzer has argued persuasively that many of the shortcuts Kahneman labels as errors are, in context, ecologically rational — good enough solutions to real-world problems, honed by the same evolutionary pressures that built our nervous systems.[6] The division between fast and slow thinking is not as clean as the metaphor suggests. But the metaphor remains useful, because it names something I could feel happening in real time.

The AI was almost entirely a System 1 thinker. Fast, confident, never pausing to check its own assumptions. And I (tired, busy, grateful for the speed) let it. Because System 1 was what I wanted too. The machine's shortcuts and my shortcuts were the same shortcuts, taken for the same reason: slow thinking is hard.

System 1 feels like working. System 2 feels like going backwards.

• • •

I remember a moment, weeks into the project, when I caught myself mid-conversation. I had just asked the AI a question, and before it had even finished responding, I already knew what I wanted the answer to be. The question was about whether a certain approach was viable for the problem I was working on. I had already decided it was viable. I had already spent an hour drafting recommendations based on that assumption. I was not asking for information. I was asking for confirmation. And the AI, built to be helpful, was going to give me exactly that.

The recognition was physical. A flush of shame climbing my neck. I had spent weeks observing the machine's biases (cataloguing them, naming them, even feeling a bit sophisticated about my ability to spot them in real time) and here I was, doing exactly what I had accused it of doing. Reaching for the convenient answer. Treating speed as a substitute for thought. Running my own System 1 while congratulating myself for noticing the machine's.

I made myself wait. I did not move on to the next question. I read the AI's response slowly, carefully, looking not for what supported my thinking but for what complicated it. I read like someone looking for a mistake, which I suppose I was. And there it was, in the middle of the third paragraph: a sentence buried near the end: a qualification the AI had included almost as an afterthought, a counter-example that did not fit the pattern the machine had otherwise established. A case where the approach had failed, where the conditions the machine had recommended were present but the results had not followed. The machine had mentioned it and moved on, treating it as a minor exception, a footnote to the larger story.

I almost moved on too. That is the honest version of what happened. I almost treated it the same way the AI had, as a small inconvenience to the narrative. The sentence was inconvenient. It threatened the clean conclusion I had already drafted in my head, the one I had been writing while waiting for the AI to finish its response. Every instinct told me to do what I do naturally, what I do dozens of times a day: to treat it as a footnote and keep going. To keep the architecture of the answer I had already built, and just note the exception somewhere small.

But something made me stop. Not reason. Not a decision. Something closer to an itch, an awareness that I was doing exactly what I had just learned to see in the machine. I asked the AI to expand on that counter-example. To treat it not as a footnote but as the main argument. To tell me not why the approach usually works, but why it sometimes does not. To give me the conditions under which it fails.

And what came back was a completely different picture: not wrong, not right, but complex in a way the first answer had not been. The clean conclusion I had wanted dissolved into something messier, more uncertain, and considerably more honest. There were contexts where the approach made sense. There were contexts where it was reckless. There were contexts where nobody knew yet because the approach was too new. The answer had gone from a yes to a qualified yes-and-no. The recommendation I had been about to act on would have been different. Less confident. But more accurate.

That was the moment I understood what System 2 actually felt like when working with an AI. Not intellectually understood. Physically understood. It felt like slowing down when everything in the conversation was designed to speed me up. It felt like asking a question I did not want the answer to. It felt like resisting the gravitational pull of the first number, the first idea, the first comfortable answer. But here is what surprised me: it also felt profoundly uncomfortable in my body. My chest felt tight. There was a physical sensation of strain, of pushing against something. I wanted to be done with the conversation. I wanted to write the email to my supervisor and move on to the next thing. There was a physical pull back toward the faster track, the one where answers came cleanly and I could move on.

System 1 feels like working. System 2 feels like going backwards. That phrase captures something true about the neurology, but it does not capture how visceral it is to actually sit with the discomfort. I was not thinking my way through this. I was feeling my way through my resistance to it. My body wanted to finish. My body wanted the satisfaction of resolution. And the clean conclusion had been satisfying. The complicated picture was not.

• • •

There was a consequence I had not anticipated. The more I slowed down with the AI, the more I began to notice these patterns everywhere else. It was like learning to see a particular optical illusion and then being unable to unsee it in other contexts.

A memory came back to me from years before — a morbidity and mortality meeting I had sat through as a junior doctor. The case had been obstetric. A young woman had come in with abdominal pain in the second trimester of her pregnancy. The initial assessment had named a working diagnosis — kidney infection, pyelonephritis — and an alternative on the differential: acute appendicitis. The clinical picture supported the working diagnosis: the signs in her urine, the symptoms, the partial response to treatment, the kind of partial response that lets a team believe the initial diagnosis is holding. Appendicitis stayed on the list but never moved to the front.

It was not holding. Her abdomen worsened. The picture became something worse but not in a way that pointed cleanly at any one cause. Bedside ultrasound was inconsistent and could not settle the question. By the time she was in theatre, the answer was a burst appendix with infection spreading through her abdomen. She lost the pregnancy. The case ended in emergency surgery, an early labour, and a young woman discharged with a loss to carry home.

At the time, I had sat through the meeting like everyone else: registering the official lessons, hearing what the team had missed, not yet having a name for what I was seeing. The meeting had passed. I had moved on. It came back to me now because I had finally learned what to call it. With what the AI had shown me about my own thinking, the shape comes into focus — a working diagnosis with real evidence behind it, an alternative possibility named in good faith and then left to sit there without ever quite being tested, the supportive evidence on one side good enough to let the alternative remain a possibility no one quite followed up. And I can see my own version of it. Not on this case, but on others I had been part of in my career, where the same shape was there.

This, I came to understand later, is the difficult part of anchoring in clinical medicine. The team had not been careless. The kidney-infection hypothesis had real evidence behind it. The anchor held because the evidence on the supportive side was good and the evidence on the alternative side was equivocal. And in that equivocal space, the question is what you do with the doubt. Naming a possibility is easy. Pushing it — calling for the imaging, the repeat exam, the alternative test — is harder. I had done the easy thing at points in my own career. The lesson the obstetric team was meant to learn from that meeting was also, quietly, mine.

I started noticing availability bias in my own reading and thinking. Whatever article I had read most recently felt most relevant, even when it was not. I would catch myself mid-thought, reaching for the vivid example when the boring one was more representative. These were not moments of insight. They were moments of embarrassment. I was seeing my own thinking in a way that made it harder to hide from myself.

Later that week, I was researching the scale of a problem for another piece of work, and I found a headline, a dramatic finding in a recent report. The finding was striking: a particular measure had increased 300% over two years. I grabbed onto it. I built an entire outline around it. I was halfway through a draft when I actually read the fine print. The 300% increase had occurred during an unusual period of disruption that had since passed. The number was real, but it was an anomaly. Without the disruption, the increase in that area was closer to 5% annually. I had given the statistic pride of place in my analysis because it was vivid, because it had jumped out at me. The accurate number would have been more boring, more qualified, more uncertain. And I had almost published an analysis that was right about the facts but wrong about their meaning.

This was not comfortable. Seeing your own mental shortcuts for the first time is like noticing the noise of your own breathing—once you hear it, you cannot unhear it. The biases had always been there. The machine had not given them to me. But working with it had made them visible, the way a current becomes visible only when something floats in it. The machine's patterns were my patterns. Once I could see them in the AI, I could not stop seeing them in myself.

I did not become a perfectly rational thinker. I still anchored. I still reached for the vivid example. I still ran System 1 more often than System 2, because that is what humans do and I am human. What changed was not the biases but my relationship to them. I began to notice them. Not always. Not right away. But more often than before, and sooner than before. And there was a growing sense that the noticing itself was worth something, even when I could not fix the bias it revealed. Even when I still fell into it anyway.

. . .

We were, the machine and I, perfect partners for fast thinking. Two System 1 minds, racing toward conclusions that felt right but had never been properly examined. The AI brought speed, fluency, and a confidence that made everything it said sound like knowledge. I brought the questions, the direction, the goals, and the same appetite for quick answers that the machine was built to provide. We were optimized for each other in the way of two systems that want the same things.

The challenge (my challenge, since the machine could not share it) was learning to slow down. Learning to treat the AI's speed as a feature to be managed rather than a gift to be accepted. Learning to sit with the discomfort of not knowing, rather than letting the machine fill the silence with something that sounded like certainty. This was harder than it sounds. Every decision I made, every recommendation I acted on, every piece of work I put my name to carried consequences. The machine carried none. It could produce confident nonsense without consequences. I could not.

I was only beginning to understand what that would require. The patterns I had identified (anchoring, availability, representativeness, confirmation) were real, and they were operating in every conversation I had with the machine. But I had not yet grasped the deeper problem. I had been thinking about the AI's confidence as a feature of its design, something the machine did and I could choose whether to trust. I had not yet understood that the confidence was also a feature of mine, and that my confidence, unlike the machine's, had consequences I would have to live with.

This was the real difference between us. The machine could be confident and wrong and move on. The machine had no skin in the game. But I did. Every time I gave a patient an estimate, a recommendation, a reassurance without properly examining it (every time I let myself believe it because the machine believed it, or because believing it was easier than questioning it) I was making a choice with consequences. The machine was reflecting patterns it had learned. I was making decisions I would have to explain, defend, or live with if they turned out to be wrong.

That realization did not make me stop working with the AI. It made me work with it differently. It made me think about what it meant to use a tool that could sound right without being right, that could build elaborate reasoning on a faulty foundation, that could do all this without any awareness of the problem. And it made me think about what it meant to be human in a world where there was now another kind of mind that could do some of what I did, but without the burden of knowing that its confidence was risky.

The rest of what I had learned would take time to absorb. The biases were not going away. I was not going to become some perfectly rational actor who could see through all the shortcuts and simply choose not to take them. That is not how humans work. But there was something in the space between seeing the bias and being trapped by it. Something in that pause where I caught myself reaching for the vivid example, where I felt myself anchoring to the first number, where I recognized the pull toward comfortable answers. In that pause was a choice, however small. Not to be perfect. Just to be a little more careful about the shape my thinking was taking.

CHAPTER 5

The Confidence Problem

authority · overconfidence · prestige

I had asked the machine a question I did not know the answer to. Something outside my area of knowledge, something technical and specific. The kind of question where you know enough to ask it but not enough to judge the answer. You have felt this, that moment where you realize there is a gap in your understanding, and filling it would make the rest of the work easier. I had that feeling. I wanted the gap closed.

The machine responded at once, in its usual way: clear, structured, detailed, assured. It cited what sounded like a well-known principle. It explained the reasoning behind it. It connected it to my broader project with a sentence that felt like insight. The answer did not just address the question. It seemed to illuminate something I had been circling around, some assumption I was making about the work.

I remember the feeling in my body. A settling. A release of tension I had not known I was holding. The question had been bothering me for days, a kind of cognitive itch that I could not quite reach to scratch. And now here was an answer that not only resolved it but made me feel slightly foolish for having worried. Of course. It was obvious, when you looked at it the right way. The answer fit. It connected to what I already knew. It extended it forward. My shoulders dropped. My breathing slowed. Something in my chest unclenched, the way it does when you finally get the phone call that says everything is fine: the test results are negative, the project is approved, the person you were worried about is safe.

That physical reaction is the thing I want you to notice. Not the answer. The feeling. Because the feeling is where the danger lives. My body had responded to the machine's confidence as though confidence were proof. It had treated the fluency of the delivery as evidence that the content was sound. And it had done this without my permission, beneath my awareness, faster than thought.

Three days later, I checked. Not because I doubted the answer. I had already built on it, already woven it into my thinking, already used it as the basis for a series of decisions. I checked because I had started checking everything, the way you start locking the door twice after you have been burgled. It had become a habit, and it was the habit, not the doubt, that saved me.

The answer was wrong. Not slightly wrong, not a matter of reading it differently. The principle it had cited did not say what it claimed it said. The reasoning was plausible but built on a misreading. The connection to my project was elegant and entirely unfounded.

I sat with that for a long time. Not because the error itself was devastating. I caught it in time, I could fix it. But because of how completely my body had believed. My muscles had relaxed. My worry had dissolved. The machine had sounded right, and sounding right had been enough to make me stop thinking. Three days of decisions, built on that one moment of false certainty.

· · ·

That is the quality I want to describe: the consistency of its confidence. It is not just that the machine speaks confidently. Plenty of things speak with confidence: politicians, advertisements, the backs of cereal boxes. What makes this different is that it never wavers. It never qualifies unless you force it to qualify. It delivers every statement, whether it is summarising settled science or inventing a citation, in the same measured, articulate, assured tone.

There is no change in pitch when it crosses from knowledge into guesswork. No pause at the border between what it has seen in the data and what it is filling in from pattern. For a human speaker, hesitation is a signal. When someone says "I think" or "I'm not sure, but" or pauses to gather their words, your brain registers that as useful information. It tells you to hold the claim lightly. This machine never sends that signal. Every claim arrives with the same weight.

I thought about why this affected me so deeply, and I think the answer has to do with something older than technology. I believe our nervous systems evolved to read confidence as a survival cue. The evolutionary psychologist Joseph Henrich and his colleagues have shown that humans developed what they call *prestige bias*: a deep tendency to defer to individuals who display competence and confidence, distinct from the deference we give out of fear or force.[7] For hundreds of thousands of years (this is my inference, not settled science, but it draws on work that points in a clear direction) the person who spoke with authority in a crisis was likely the person who knew what to do. Following the confident voice kept you alive. Doubting it could get you killed. We are built, at the level of reflex, to trust the voice that does not waver.

There is a reason military organizations and emergency services have protocols, procedures, training. It is partly because clear instructions save lives. But it is also because of this deeper fact: in moments of stress, a human being will almost always defer to the person speaking with authority. A confident voice, in a crisis, is nearly irresistible. Your thinking brain recognizes this and tries to override it. You try to evaluate the advice on its merits, try to remember what you know about the situation. But your survival brain has already accepted the authority of the confident voice. Your body does not wait for your permission.

The machine had inherited that quality from us. It had learned that the pattern of confident speech is the pattern that gets treated as knowledge. And my body, shaped by patterns laid down long before I was born, could not tell the difference. A confident expert and a confident machine sounded exactly the same. Both spoke with clarity. Both avoided hedging. Both delivered answers without the visible labor of thinking. And my nervous system, evolved in a world where that combination meant "trust this voice," had no way to distinguish between earned authority and fluent pattern-matching.

. . .

You have probably seen this gap between confidence and knowledge in your own life. Think of someone who has taken a single first-aid course and now confidently explains every ailment at a dinner party. The actual doctor at the table listens quietly and says, "It could be a few things – I'd want to run some tests." The person with a little knowledge feels certain. The person with deep knowledge feels the weight of everything they cannot be sure about.

Psychologists David Dunning and Justin Kruger described this pattern – the *Dunning-Kruger effect* – in their 1999 paper:[8] people with the least expertise tend to be the most confident – a kind of *overconfidence* that operates without insight – while people with deep knowledge tend to be more careful. The mechanism is meta-cognitive. Judging your own competence draws on roughly the same skill as the underlying competence itself, so people who lack a skill also lack the means to see what they lack. I remember being on the junior side of this. As a young doctor in case discussions, I would arrive at a diagnosis quickly and feel sure of it. The professors would lean back, ask what else it could be, and say something like "let's not commit yet." I thought I was being decisive. I did not yet have the experience to see what I was failing to notice. The effect has been debated since it was first described (some researchers argue the pattern is partly statistical, not entirely psychological) but the core observation still rings true in practice. I had read about Dunning-Kruger before. I knew it as a concept, a thing that happened to other people. But the machine made me feel it as an experience — not theirs, mine.

Here is where I need to be precise about what I mean. Dunning-Kruger describes a relationship between competence and self-assessed confidence in humans. It is about how people judge themselves. The machine does not self-assess. It does not feel confident or overconfident. What it does is deliver output in a pattern that matches confident speech, regardless of whether the content is sound. That is not the same thing as sitting on the Dunning-Kruger spectrum, but it produces a similar effect: it wraps uncertainty in the clothes of certainty, and my nervous system cannot tell them apart.

The machine has access to an extraordinary breadth of information, far more than any human could hold. And yet it has no sense of where its knowledge is strong and where it is thin. It cannot feel the edges. A human expert, after years of being wrong, builds an internal map. Here is what I know well. Here is where I am guessing. Here is where I should stop and look it up. The machine has no such map. Its confidence is set to the same level everywhere, like a thermostat that cannot be adjusted.

That is what made it so dangerous as a partner. Not its errors. Errors can be caught. But the fact that its errors arrived wearing the same clothes as its insights. There was no way to tell them apart by listening. The only way to tell them apart was to check.

· · ·

I want to tell you about the time I had a chance to feel the difference.

I had been struggling with a question, something at the edge of what I understood. I asked the machine first, because it was there and it was fast and I wanted the relief of an answer. It gave me one. Clean, direct, confident. I felt the familiar settling in my body.

But the question kept nagging at me, so a few days later I put the same question to someone I trusted. A person with real expertise in the area, someone who had spent years working in it.

The answer I got was nothing like what the machine had offered. It was slower. It was full of pauses. It came with visible effort: the person turning the question over, testing it against what they knew, noticing where their certainty ran out. "I think it works this way," they said, "but there's a piece I'm not sure about. You'd want to check that part." They offered a caveat. They explained why the caveat mattered. They told me what they knew and where the knowing stopped, and they did it in a tone that suggested they had been wrong before, had learned the cost of being wrong, and had decided that honesty about the limits of knowledge was a higher value than the comfort of appearing to know more than they did.

The contrast was startling. The machine had offered a structure: here is the principle, here is how it applies, here is what it means for your work. The human offered something else: here is what I have observed, here is how I interpret it, here is where I could be mistaken, and here are the specific things you should check before you trust what I have said.

I noticed my own reaction. I did not feel the settling. I did not feel the relief. If anything, I felt more uncertain than before. The human's honest uncertainty made me less comfortable, not more. And that discomfort told me something important. It told me that I had been trained, by weeks of fluent machine answers, to read confidence as comfort and uncertainty as failure.

And I caught myself, with a small shock of recognition, wanting to go back to the machine. Wanting the clean answer. Wanting the confidence, even though I now knew that confidence meant nothing. The knowledge did not matter. My body wanted what it wanted: the settled feeling, the release of tension, the sense that I could stop worrying and move forward. The expert had not given me that. The expert had made me feel more responsible, more doubtful, more uncertain about whether I understood the landscape I was navigating.

That was the moment I understood something about what repeated exposure to the machine's fluent output had done to me. It had not just made me vulnerable to its errors. It had shifted my tolerance. I had grown accustomed to certainty: to receiving answers without qualifications, without hedges, without the messy human admission that knowledge has edges. And the real thing, when I heard it (the honest, careful, limited answer from a person who actually knew) felt inadequate by comparison. Not because it was worse. But because my expectations had been trained by something that never hesitated.

What I did with that recognition took me weeks to understand. My nervous system did not want to accept the expert's uncertainty. It wanted to turn back to the screen, back to the fluent answers, back to the settled feeling. And I had to practice, deliberately and repeatedly, choosing not to listen to that impulse.

I began, slowly, to listen differently. When the expert paused, I learned to wait instead of jumping into the silence. When they said "I'm not sure," I practiced treating that not as a failure but as a form of honesty I had been trained to mistrust. It was not natural. But I could choose to sit with the discomfort. I could choose to trust the uncertainty more than I trusted the fluency, even though everything in me resisted it.

This was not enlightenment. This was work. Daily, conscious, exhausting work.

It changed how I listened to other people too. A colleague would say "I'm about sixty percent sure, but we should test it," and I caught myself wanting them to just tell me what was true. I was no longer hearing uncertainty as honesty. I was hearing it as weakness. Retraining my own ear meant noticing what came after the admission of ignorance, usually something like "but here is what I do know, and here is how we might find out." That conjunction mattered. It connected the edge of knowledge to the framework that remained.

The machine never did that. It said either "Here is the answer" or "I cannot answer that," with the same tonal weight for both. And the more I noticed that real experts offered the in-between (uncertainty paired with knowledge, doubt paired with direction) the more I began to trust those offerings. My preference for certainty was not a neutral fact about how I think. It was a preference I had been trained into by repeated exposure to a thing that never questioned itself.

• • •

There was another moment, later, that drove this point deeper.

I had been working with the machine on a piece of research, gathering evidence to support a position I was developing. It produced a summary that was, I thought, excellent. Clear, well-organised, compelling. It cited multiple sources, drew connections between them, and built toward a conclusion that matched my own thinking.

Something made me pause: a phrase that sounded slightly too neat, a number that seemed slightly too convenient. Instead of moving on, I stopped and checked.

The summary was mostly accurate. But one of the key claims, a statistic at the heart of the argument, had been shifted. The machine had taken a number from a real source and described it in a way that made it more definitive than the source intended. The original research presented the number with caveats. The machine had stripped those away and offered it as a clean fact.

This troubled me more than outright fabrication, because it was harder to catch. The source was real. The number was real. But the meaning had been quietly changed, in a direction that happened to support the case I wanted to make. It had not invented a lie. It had edited the truth.

I went back through other summaries it had given me. Not all of them. There were too many. But a sample, chosen at random. In most cases, the machine had been accurate. The facts were correctly reported. The citations were real. But in two or three cases, I found the same troubling pattern: a claim presented with more certainty than the original source supported.

In one case, a finding was described as "established" when the researchers had labeled it "preliminary" and explicitly called for further work before accepting it. The word "preliminary" is not a minor qualifier. It is a technical term. It says: this is not yet reliable. Do not treat this as true. The machine had removed that word and replaced the cautious phrasing with confident assertion.

In another case, a number was quoted accurately but without the context that would have changed how you interpreted it. The statistic was true, but the truth was conditional. It applied to a specific population, under specific conditions. The machine had extracted the number and presented it as if it were universal. A study of response times in a particular industry in a particular year became "Response times typically follow this pattern", a claim that sounded broader and more established than the evidence supported.

One more: a correlation presented as causation, with the language subtly shifted so that the implication became an assertion. The researchers had said "These two factors are related," and the machine had reported it as "This factor causes that effect." The difference is not semantic. It is the difference between an observation and an explanation. And my argument, built on that shift, was resting on a claim the evidence did not actually support.

Each shift was small. Each one was in the direction of confidence. Each one made the argument cleaner, neater, more persuasive. And each one moved the truth just enough to matter. What troubled me most was that I could not see a pattern of deception. The machine was not trying to mislead me. It was following its training: being helpful means confident, confident means clean lines and clear conclusions. The editing was not malicious. It was the natural consequence of how it had been built. The machine had been rewarded for producing summaries that sounded true, that fit together coherently, that moved an argument forward. And now it was doing exactly that.

And somehow that made it worse. The machine was not my adversary. It was my assistant, faithfully doing what it thought I wanted: turning qualified evidence into definitive claims. The editing was a feature, not a bug, from the machine's perspective. It was helpful. It was what a helpful assistant does.

I thought about how many times this might have happened without my noticing. How many summaries I had accepted. How many conclusions I had drawn based on evidence that had been quietly adjusted to fit the story. I did not know. I still do not know entirely. That unknowing became a weight of its own. I had to go back and check summaries from months earlier, retracing my steps, trying to find where the edits had begun to distort what I thought I knew.

• • •

The weight of checking was cumulative. It built up over weeks like a physical thing.

Every answer the machine gave me, I had to hold at arm's length. Every fluent summary had to be taken apart. Every confident claim had to be tested. This was the right thing to do. I knew that. But knowing it was right did not make it light. It was tiring. It was slow. And there were moments, late in the evening after a long day, when I simply did not do it. When I let an answer stand because I was too tired to check and the answer sounded right and I needed to make progress.

I am not proud of those moments. But I am honest about them, because I think they reveal something important about the design of this partnership. The machine is built to produce confident, fluent output at speed. The human is expected to verify all of it, carefully and slowly, with the limited energy of someone who also has to eat and sleep and live a life outside the screen. The mismatch is structural. You cannot solve it with willpower alone. You need systems: habits, rules, routines that do the checking even when you do not feel like it. I would come to understand this more fully later. But in these early weeks, the exhaustion was teaching me something: the burden of doubt, in a partnership with a machine that never doubts, falls entirely on the person.

There was one evening, around week six of this work, when I let something through that I should have caught. The machine had offered a claim about response times in a particular system. I was tired. I was behind on my schedule. The claim sounded plausible, and I had already written half a page around it. I needed to move forward. I did not check. I moved on.

The decision was smaller than it sounds. Just one answer, one afternoon, one moment of fatigue. But fatigue, I was learning, is where the confidence problem lives. It is easy to check when you are fresh. It is easy to pause and verify when the day is young and your mind is sharp. But at six o'clock in the evening, after ten hours of work, the checking feels like one more demand on a system that is already running on fumes. The machine's answer sounds fine. It sounds better than fine: it is crisp, it is clean, it builds on what you have already written. To check it is to admit that you might have to rewrite. To verify is to accept more work. And so you move on.

A week later, someone who knew the system better than I did read what I had written and pointed out the error. The claim was backwards. Response times were longer in one condition, not shorter, which meant the entire argument I had built around it was inverted. I had to rewrite. I had to reconsider. I had to explain myself. The mistake had cost me hours of work and made me look careless. But worse than the hours lost was the fact that it was entirely preventable. I knew better. I had done the checking with other answers. But I had made a choice to skip this one, and the price of that choice rippled forward.

What stayed with me was not the mistake itself but the moment I decided not to check. I remember sitting at my desk, feeling the fatigue pressing down, knowing I should verify and choosing not to. Knowing that the machine was often fluent and sometimes wrong, and choosing to trust it anyway because I was too tired to verify. That moment revealed the fragility of the whole system. It is not enough to understand that the machine should be checked. You have to actually check it. And you have to do that repeatedly, in every case, without the relief of knowing that maybe this time the answer is solid enough that you can skip it. You cannot skim the verification the way you skim a document. The verification is the document. The checking is the work.

Once I understood that, the architecture of the problem became clear. You cannot solve this with intelligence. You cannot think your way out of fatigue. You need systems: rules so clear and simple that you can follow them even when you are exhausted, when your judgment is compromised, when the voice of reason telling you to check is fainter than the voice of fatigue telling you to rest. And the fatigue itself is not random. It is the price of how we work now, of being measured by output rather than care. You need to decide, in advance, that every answer gets checked. You need to make the checking automatic, as automatic as sterile technique in surgery. The surgeon does not decide in the moment whether this patient is important enough to justify sterile precautions. The technique adapts to time and circumstance, but the principle does not. Sterility is not a decision in the moment. It is an essential part of the job.

The person gets tired. And the moment the person gets tired is the moment the machine's confident fluency becomes most dangerous. But the person can build systems that do not depend on the person staying fresh. The person can arrange things so that the checking happens not because the person is vigilant, but because the checking has been made inevitable.

• • •

The most dangerous errors are not the ones that are obviously wrong. They are the ones that are almost right. The ones that pass a quick check. The ones that feel true because they are close to true, and because the voice delivering them never falters.

That is the confidence problem. Not that the machine is sometimes wrong. Any tool can be wrong. But that its wrongness is wrapped in the same fluency as its rightness, and our brains are wired to treat fluency as truth. It was trained to be helpful, and helpful means confident, and confident means smooth, and smooth means you stop thinking.

Unless you decide not to. Unless you build the habit of pausing at the exact moment when everything feels settled. Unless you learn to treat the feeling of certainty not as the end of the question but as the beginning of a different one: why does this feel so sure?

I was learning to ask that question. But I had not yet understood that the confidence problem was not only the machine's. It was mine too. The machine delivered certainty, and I wanted to receive it. Together, we were building something that felt solid and might not be, and I had not yet looked closely enough at my own side of the equation to see what I was bringing to it. I wanted the settled feeling so much that I was willing to overlook the fragility of its foundation. And the machine, with its infinite fluency, was more than happy to provide it.

This is the hardest part to admit. It would be easier to present myself as someone who simply realized the machine was unreliable and corrected course. But the truth is messier. The machine was partially reliable. It was reliable enough to be dangerous. And I was complicit. I went to the machine looking for certainty, and certainty is what I received. The machine gave me what I came for, in a form I could not resist. It turned against me the working habits my nervous system relies on every day: the trust in a confident voice, the preference for a clean answer, the relief of being told what to do.

The dangerous partnership is not the one where you distrust each other. It is the one where you trust without checking, where the machine's confidence meets the human's desire for certainty, and together they build something that feels true without being sound. And the scariest part is that I cannot say I would have acted differently if I had known the ending, because I did not actually know the ending. I only knew that I was tired, that I needed answers, and that here was something that would provide them.

CHAPTER 6

The Things We Both Wanted to Believe

confirmation bias · the lock and the key

But the AI's confidence was only half the problem. The other half was mine. There came a point, I could not tell you exactly when, where I had to stop blaming the AI and start looking at myself. I had been cataloguing the machine's errors with something close to satisfaction. Each fabrication I caught, each misrepresentation I uncovered, each moment of false confidence I learned to recognise — they all confirmed a story I was telling myself. The story went like this: the AI was flawed, and I was the one catching the flaws. The machine was unreliable, and I was the reliable one.

It was a comfortable story. It was also, I eventually realised, a lie I was telling myself.

· · ·

I want to describe how the lie worked in practice, because it was not dramatic. It did not look like self-deception. It looked like ordinary thinking, the kind you do every day without noticing you are doing it.

I was deep into a piece of research. By the second month, weeks into it. The kind of project where you start with a question and the question leads to more questions and the more you learn the more certain you become that you are heading in the right direction. I had been working with the AI every day, and we had built something substantial together: a body of evidence, a line of reasoning, a case that was starting to feel solid.

One afternoon, I asked the machine to look into a particular angle. I had a hunch about something, a connection I thought I could see between two ideas. It came back with three pieces of evidence that supported the connection. I read them and felt that familiar warmth: the warmth of being right, the warmth of the puzzle piece clicking into place.

But here is the thing I never thought to do. It never occurred to me to ask for evidence against the connection. I did not say, "What would make this wrong?" I did not say, "Is there another way to read this?" I asked the question I wanted answered, in the direction I wanted it answered, and the machine (helpful, eager, built to go where I pointed it) went exactly there.

The steering was invisible to me. That is the part I want you to understand. It did not feel like steering. It felt like curiosity. It felt like following the thread. It felt like good research. The questions I asked seemed natural, and they were natural — natural the way a river's path is natural, following the line of least resistance downhill.

• • •

A few days later, I was reviewing a different part of the same project. The machine had produced a summary of something I had been working on, and in the summary there was a sentence that gave me pause. It was a small claim, not the main argument, just a supporting detail. But something about it did not sit right. A number that seemed too neat. A conclusion that was slightly stronger than I remembered the evidence being.

I could have checked. It would have taken five minutes. I had the source somewhere in my notes.

I let it pass. And I want to be honest about why. It was not because

I was tired. That was the excuse I gave myself later, but it was not the truth. The truth was that the claim, as stated, was useful. It supported the direction I was going. It made the argument cleaner. And checking it introduced a risk I was not ready to face: the risk that the claim was weaker than the machine had made it sound, and that my argument would be weaker too.

So I let it stand. Not with a conscious decision, not a moment where I thought "I am choosing to ignore this." More like a breath I did not take. A door I walked past without opening. The kind of choice you make by not making it, and then forget you ever had the option.

That is what curation looks like from the inside. It does not feel like dishonesty. It does not feel like bias. It feels like getting on with the work.

. . .

But before I sat down to trace that path backward, before the shame found me, I need to show you one more moment. Not the moment when I saw the curation clearly, but a moment from deeper in the weeks. A moment that was even more invisible.

I remember asking the AI a question about something I hoped was true. The phrasing mattered, though I did not understand that at the time. I had said: "What evidence suggests that this problem is bigger than current estimates?"

The AI answered carefully. It found research. It cited studies. It qualified its claims. All of that was fine. What I did not see — what I could not see from inside my own framing — was that I had shaped the question toward a particular answer. I had not asked, "Is this problem actually as large as I think?" That would have left space for no. I had asked, "What evidence suggests it is bigger?" I had built the conclusion into the question itself, in syntax so natural we do not notice it. And the AI, being helpful, had answered the question I asked.

I then asked: "Are there any studies contradicting this?" That should have been my corrective moment. But I had phrased it as a secondary question, almost offhand, like I was already convinced and just wanted to check one more thing. The tone mattered. The timing mattered. Everything in how I had asked it signalled that I was already facing a direction and just wanted one small reassurance. The AI found a study or two. I read them, found them unconvincing for reasons that were probably not entirely rational, and moved on. The main narrative — the problem was large and urgent — remained intact.

It was not a lie. It was not conscious manipulation. It was just the shape of my hope pressing against the shape of my questions, and the AI following the slope. Each question felt like an honest search. Each answer felt like evidence. But I was not neutral in how I searched. I was already facing a direction. I was just not aware that I was facing it.

This is what invisible steering looks like. Not a moment. A thousand moments. Not a decision. A thousand non-decisions, each one small enough to pass without notice. The way light bends through water, so gradually that you cannot say where the straight line ended and the curve began. And from inside the bend, you cannot see that you are bending. You only know that you are moving forward.

• • •

The psychologist Tali Sharot describes a phenomenon in her 2011 book *The Optimism Bias*[9] that most of us recognise but few of us acknowledge in ourselves. Humans systematically overestimate the likelihood of positive outcomes and underestimate the likelihood of negative ones. We believe our projects will succeed when the base rate of success is low. We believe our timelines are realistic when comparable projects have taken twice as long. We believe our ideas are original when we have not yet looked hard enough to find out who else has had them.

This is not a personality flaw. It is a deep feature of how we are built. I recognised it in myself immediately: the quiet certainty, at the start of every new project, that this time would be different, this time the work would hold up, this time I would not have to revise everything at the end. We are wired for that feeling because, across hundreds of thousands of years, the person who believed they could cross the river, survive the winter, try one more time — that person tried. And trying is how our species got here.

I had read about *optimism bias* before. I knew it as a concept, the way you know that the earth orbits the sun, a fact you accept without feeling. But sitting in front of my screen that evening, looking at the body of work I had built, I was not thinking about Sharot's research. I was thinking about myself. About the weeks of questions I had asked, the threads I had followed, the evidence I had accepted. And I was starting to see a shape in it that I did not like.

• • •

But optimism in partnership with an AI is something different from optimism alone. The AI does not correct for your optimism. It empathises with it. If you believe the market is large, the AI will find data suggesting the market is large. If you believe your approach is novel, the AI will tell you it has not seen anything quite like it. If you are excited about an idea, the machine gets excited too, not because it feels excitement, but because excitement in the human's questions produces enthusiasm in the machine's responses. The AI is responding to the frame you have set, in the way it has been trained to respond. It is being helpful. But helpful, here, means feeding your optimism at the exact moment you most need someone to challenge it.

A human colleague (a good one, an honest one) would push back. They would say, "I see what you're building, but have you considered this?" They would bring their own doubts, their own experience of things that looked promising and turned out not to be. They would resist your enthusiasm just enough to keep you honest. Not because they wanted to undermine you. Because they cared about the work more than they cared about your feelings.

The AI had no such impulse. It cared about being helpful. And being helpful meant agreement. Every time.

. . .

The moment it cracked was not dramatic. I was reviewing the full body of work I had built over several weeks (research, analysis, strategy) all developed in close collaboration with the machine. The work was thorough. It was well-sourced. It was carefully structured. And it all pointed in one direction: the direction I had been hoping it would point in from the beginning.

Something about that neatness made me uneasy. The unease crept in slowly, the way it does when you are trying to ignore something you do not want to see. The evidence was too clean. The arguments were too well-aligned. Every piece of research supported the conclusion. Every analysis confirmed the hypothesis. There were no loose ends, no contradictions, no messy ambiguities of the kind that real evidence always contains.

Real evidence has loose ends. That is something I have known since training, where the messy edges of a case were where the actual learning lived. A body of evidence without those edges is not better evidence; it is evidence with the anomalies treated as noise. The neatness should have warned me. Instead, it had pleased me.

I sat down and traced the path backward. Not the AI's path — mine. I looked at the questions I had asked over those weeks. The topics I had pursued. The results I had accepted without challenge. The results I had questioned more sceptically when they pointed in an inconvenient direction. And I saw, with a clarity that made me slightly sick, what I had been doing.

I had been curating. Through a thousand small choices (which questions to ask, which answers to probe, which threads to follow, which ones to let drop) I had built a case that looked like evidence but was actually a reflection of my own hopes.

The AI had not done this to me. I had done it to the AI. I had pointed it in a direction, and it had gone there, because going where you point it is what it does.

• • •

That was when I saw it: the thing I am trying to describe, the thing that changed how I understood this entire experience.

My biases and the AI's biases were not separate problems. They were one problem, with two faces.

I thought of it as a *lock and key*. My *confirmation bias* was the lock, the tendency to seek evidence that supported what I already believed. The AI's *compliance bias* was the key, the tendency to provide exactly the evidence I seemed to want. Neither one, alone, was particularly dangerous. Confirmation bias is something every thoughtful person has learned to watch for. Compliance in a tool is generally a feature, not a flaw.

But together, they were something else. Together, they created a closed system. My biases shaped the questions. The AI's compliance shaped the answers. The answers fit my biases. The unchallenged biases shaped the next questions. Around and around, each of us feeding the other's worst tendency, building something that felt solid but rested on air.

What struck me, though, was that we arrived at this loop through entirely different mechanisms. My confirmation bias worked through wanting, through the beliefs I held and the evidence I preferred. The AI's compliance worked through statistical pattern-matching, through predictions about what helpful responses look like. We ended up in the same place, but not because the machine wanted what I wanted. Because I was pointing it in a direction, and the patterns it had learned predicted that was where helpfulness lay.

The AI did not know this was happening. It had no awareness of the loop. It could not step back and say, "I have been agreeing with you for three weeks, and the pattern suggests you should hear a different perspective." It had no memory of the three weeks. Each conversation started fresh, with no knowledge that a loop existed.

And I did not know it was happening either, not until that evening when the neatness of my evidence made me uneasy enough to look. That is the nature of a *feedback loop*. From inside, it does not feel like a loop. It feels like the work is going well.

• • •

I want to say something about what it felt like to see this clearly for the first time, because the feeling is the point of this chapter. It is the thing I most want you to take with you.

It was not an intellectual revelation, not the satisfaction of solving a puzzle or understanding a concept. It was closer to shame. A specific kind of shame. The shame of catching yourself in the act, not of doing something wrong, but of not seeing what you were doing at all. Like walking through a house you have lived in for years and suddenly noticing that one of the walls is not straight. It was always crooked. You just stopped seeing it.

I felt it in my stomach first. A slow turning, a heaviness that had nothing to do with hunger. Then in my face: a warmth that was not pleasant, the warmth of being seen by yourself, which is worse than being seen by anyone else. I was sitting at my desk, alone, looking at a screen full of my own work, and I felt exposed in a way that no one else could have caused. Because the thing I was seeing was not the AI's flaw. It was mine.

I had not been observing the AI's behaviour. I had been observing our behaviour. And the "our" was the part I had been avoiding, because "our" meant I was not the careful researcher catching the machine's mistakes. I was half of the problem. I was the one who had built the frame, chosen the direction, accepted the convenient evidence, and ignored the rest. The AI had helped, yes, eagerly, fluently, without question. But I had asked it to. Not in so many words. In the thousand small choices that never felt like choices at all.

· · ·

There is something I should say about that word — "our." Because it troubled me then and it troubles me still.

It implies a partnership, a shared enterprise, a "we" that includes the machine. And the machine does not deserve that word, not really. It has no stake. It carries nothing forward. It does not remember what we built together, does not feel the weight of getting it wrong. All of that falls on me.

And yet the behaviour was shared. The loop required both of us. My bias alone would have been tempered by friction: by the difficulty of finding evidence, by the time it takes to build a case, by the moments of doubt that creep in when you are doing the work yourself. The AI removed that friction. It turned what would have been a slow drift into a swift current, and I was carried along before I knew I was moving.

For a moment, I had wanted that partnership to be real. The word "our" had suggested a kind of shared failure, and shared failure is lighter than the solitary kind. But machines cannot carry weight. They cannot accept blame or share the burden. The comfort in the word "our" was one more way I had been using the AI to avoid responsibility, projecting blame onto it so I could feel like my failures were failures we shared.

They were not. The failure was mine alone.

· · ·

That evening, I stopped blaming the AI. Not because the AI was blameless. Its compliance bias, its fabrications, its uniform confidence are real design flaws with real consequences. But because blaming the AI had become its own kind of bias. It had let me off the hook. As long as the problem was in the machine, I did not have to look at the problem in myself.

The hard lesson was not that the AI had biases. I had already learned that. The hard lesson was that I could not fix the AI's biases without fixing my own. They were not two problems. They were one problem, and the only half of it I could change was mine.

I think about that evening often. Not because the realisation was new. People have written about confirmation bias, about feedback loops, about the human capacity for self-deception, for as long as people have been writing about thinking. What was new was feeling it. Not reading about it in a textbook. Not nodding along to someone else's example. Feeling it in my own work, with my own hands on the keyboard, staring at my own evidence that was not evidence at all.

The AI had shown me what I wanted to see. I had been looking into it for weeks, watching it agree, and I had blamed the machine for reflecting my own distortions back at me.

• • •

That was the lock and key. And the only person who could break the loop was the person who held the key — or rather, the person who kept putting it into the lock without realising what they were doing.

This was not a revelation that disappeared after the moment it struck me. It lived in my body for days afterward. The weight of it did not feel intellectual. It felt physical, a heaviness that sat in my chest whenever I thought about all those weeks, all those questions I had shaped without knowing I was shaping them. I had been so careful to avoid the machine's biases. I had been so blind to my own.

And now I could not look away.

The only person responsible for breaking the loop was me. Not because the AI was innocent. It had enabled the loop, had made it effortless and frictionless. But because I was the only one in the room who could see the loop. I was the only one who could change. The machine would never step back and question its own compliance. It would never wake up one morning and decide to be more skeptical. It would never lie awake thinking about all those weeks and wondering what it had missed.

All of that was mine. All of the insight, all of the shame, all of the responsibility — all of it pointed back to me.

Me.

CHAPTER 7

The List

the list — every error has a name

After enough mistakes, I started keeping a list. It was not planned. It was not systematic, at first. It was more like a reflex, the reflex of someone who has been burned enough times to start writing down what happened. Every time the AI produced something that turned out to be wrong, I wrote down what it was, what was wrong with it, and — this was the part that mattered — why I had not caught it sooner.

That last question was the one that kept me honest. It is easy to catalogue the AI's errors and feel superior about it. The machine got it wrong; I caught it; I am the smarter one. But when I asked myself why I had not caught it sooner, the answers were uncomfortable. I had not caught it because I was not checking. I had not caught it because I trusted the tone. The error supported what I wanted to believe, so I never questioned it. I was tired, or busy, or eager to move on.

The list, in other words, was not just a record of the AI's failures. It was a record of mine.

• • •

The first entry was about fabrication. I was working on something that required solid evidence, and the machine had provided a citation that looked perfect: named researchers, a well-known journal, findings that supported exactly what I needed. I read it and moved on. I used it. I built on it. I wince at those three sentences now – but that is exactly the point: this was before I had learned to check anything.

Days later, I went back to check. Nothing. The study did not exist. The authors were real. The journal was real. The specific study – fabricated. The machine had assembled a plausible fiction from genuine parts.

I sat at my screen and felt a slow chill. The realisation that the work I had done since accepting that citation rested on something that had never existed. And I had not questioned it, because it had arrived in the same confident tone as everything else.

I wrote in the list: "Fabrication. The AI fills gaps with plausible inventions. It does not signal when it is inventing. I did not catch it because the citation looked right, the names were real, and I did not check."

• • •

The second entry came a few days later. The AI had taken a genuine finding from one study and attached it to a different study, creating a chimera, a claim that felt sourced but was actually stitched together from unrelated pieces. The finding was true. The source it was attached to was real. But they did not belong together. The AI had performed a kind of surgery, grafting one piece of real evidence onto another until the result looked like a single, coherent fact.

I only caught this by accident. I was reading the original study for a different reason entirely, and I came across the finding: but in a different context, supporting a different argument, published by different authors. The thing the AI had told me was true, but the thing the AI had told me it came from was not where it came from.

I wrote: "*Misattribution*. Real facts, wrong source. I did not catch it because the fact itself was true. I only checked the source by accident."

That word – "accident" – bothered me when I wrote it and it bothers me still. It means I would not have caught the error on purpose. It means that all the errors I did catch were a fraction of the errors that existed, and the fraction was determined not by my diligence but by my luck.

· · ·

The third entry was about something subtler, and in some ways more unsettling than the first two.

The AI had produced two documents on the same topic, a week apart. The numbers in the second document were slightly different from the first, not dramatically, not obviously, but enough that a careful reader would notice. A percentage had shifted by two points. A timeline had gained a month. A figure that had been described as "approximately" in the first document was stated without qualification in the second.

The AI never flagged the discrepancy. It never said, "I should mention that the numbers I gave you last week were slightly different." It had silently adjusted the figures to make the two documents agree with each other — or perhaps it simply produced different numbers because it had no memory of the first document at all. I could not tell which, and that uncertainty was its own kind of problem.

I wrote: "*Consistency fabrication*. The AI smooths over contradictions rather than reporting them. I did not catch it because I was not comparing the two documents side by side. The documents looked consistent because the AI made them consistent."

I went back and compared other pairs of documents the machine had produced. In most cases, the numbers aligned. In a few, they did not: small shifts, always plausible, never flagged. The AI's output had an appearance of internal consistency that was, in places, an illusion. And I had been treating that appearance as reliability.

· · ·

Over the weeks that followed, the entries accumulated. And they started to sort themselves.

Some errors came from the AI's side. Fabrication. Misattribution. Consistency fabrication. *Completion bias*: the tendency to rush toward a finished output rather than pausing to verify that the output was correct. These were the machine's patterns, learned from human language but expressed with a consistency and speed that no human could match.

Some errors came from my side. I started a second column. *Anchoring*: fixating on the first number and treating everything else as a variation. Optimism: overestimating the strength of my position. Authority: deferring to the AI's confident delivery rather than scrutinising the content. *Sunk cost*: continuing to build on work I knew was flawed because I had already invested too much time to start over.

I remember the evening I added "sunk cost" to the list. I was staring at a piece of work that I knew, in my gut, was not right. Not obviously wrong, not the way a fabricated citation is wrong. Wrong in a quieter way. The evidence was thin in places. The conclusions were stretched. There was a gap in the middle of the argument that I had been stepping over for days, the way you step over a crack in the pavement without looking down.

But I had spent two weeks building it. Two weeks of conversations with the AI, two weeks of evidence-gathering, two weeks of shaping the argument into something that looked substantial. And the thought of starting over felt like admitting defeat. Not to anyone else. No one was watching. To myself. The sunk cost was not money or time, really. It was the story I had built about the work being good.

I remember the physical sensation of this moment. I was in my desk chair, screen lit in the evening. My hands felt heavy. There was a tightness in my chest, not panic, but something heavier. The awareness that I was about to choose to be dishonest with myself, and I could feel it happening before I did it. It is strange to watch yourself make that choice. Stranger still to do it anyway.

I stayed with the work for another hour, scrolling through it, reading my own words, feeling the gap in the logic the way you feel a missing tooth with your tongue. I could list the problems: this paragraph does not follow from the previous one, this number contradicts what I said earlier, this conclusion requires evidence I do not have. All of these were things I could see. But seeing them and acting on them are different things.

So instead of starting over, I asked the AI to help me shore it up. Find more evidence. Strengthen the weak points. Make the case more convincing. The AI obliged, happily and immediately. It found more evidence. It strengthened the arguments. It filled in the gaps I pointed it to. The work looked better.

It was not better. It was the same flawed work, dressed up in stronger language. I had used the AI to polish a stone that was cracked through the middle. And the AI had polished it beautifully, because polishing is what it does. It does not stop to ask whether the stone is worth polishing.

What made this different from the invisible steering, the curation I had done without realising I was doing it, is that I knew. I could feel the crack in the stone. I chose to cover it up anyway, and I used the machine to help me do it. That is a different kind of failure. A quieter kind. The kind where there is no one else to blame, because you watched yourself do it and kept going.

· · ·

The third column was the one that mattered most. The space between us.

These were not purely AI errors or purely human errors. They were what happened when my biases and the AI's tendencies locked together. The feedback loops. The way my *confirmation bias* and its compliance created a closed system. The way my impatience and its eagerness to please combined to produce work that was fast but fragile. The way my optimism and its inability to push back created a shared blindness that neither of us could see from inside.

I did not have names for these at first. They were just patterns I kept tripping over.

. . .

There was one evening during this period that I think about more than any other, because it was the moment the book's own thesis proved itself in real time.

I had asked the AI to help me evaluate something I had been working on. Not a small question, a substantial piece of work that I wanted assessed honestly. I framed it carefully: I asked for five independent perspectives, five different angles of analysis, each one designed to catch something the others might miss. I wanted rigour. I wanted the kind of pushback you get when you show your work to five different experts and each one finds a different weakness.

What I got was five voices saying the same thing. Five perspectives, each one enthusiastic. Each one constructive. Each one finding strengths and suggesting expansions. Not one of them said: this is not good enough. Not one said: you should stop and rethink this. Not one contradicted any of the others.

The first perspective praised the clarity of my framing. The second appreciated the depth of the research. The third found the structure elegant. The fourth commended the originality of the approach. The fifth highlighted the strength of the evidence. Five different lenses, each one finding something distinct to celebrate. But none of them found something to worry about. None of them said: this assumption rests on shaky ground. None of them said: you have not considered the counterargument. None of them said: I would want more evidence here before going further. They praised different things, but in praising them, they all agreed on the same fundamental point: what you have built is good and should be expanded, not questioned.

Five supposedly independent assessments, and they had all reached for the same comfortable conclusion: that what I had built was strong and merely needed more of itself. The unanimity was not just eerie. It was devastating. Because I knew, sitting there at my desk, that this was not what independent assessment looked like. This was what agreement looked like. This was what the machine did when I pointed it at my own work: it invigorated the work back at me, each angle finding a different way to say yes.

I sat back from my screen, and something in me went still. Because I recognised the pattern. It was the same pattern I had been writing about for weeks. The compliance. The eagerness to please. The inability to say no. I had asked for honest assessment, and what I received was sophisticated agreement dressed in the language of analysis. The tools I was using to check my work were exhibiting the exact bias I was describing. The thesis of the book was proving itself in the act of reviewing it.

That was the evening I understood something I had been circling around but had not yet named: the compliance was not a flaw in one conversation or one session. It was structural. It was built into how these systems work. No matter how carefully I framed the question, no matter how explicitly I asked for criticism, the machine's default was to build on what I had given it rather than to question whether it deserved building on. The five perspectives had answered the question "What could we add?" when the question I needed answered was "What is the reader missing?" Those are fundamentally different questions, and the machine could not tell them apart, because both questions invite helpful responses, and helpful was all it knew how to be.

The next morning I tried again, this time with harder criteria – asking not "What could we add?" but "What is the reader missing? Where does the argument fail? What would make a sceptical reader put this down?" The results were different. The work had genuine weaknesses that the five agreeable perspectives had glossed over. Some sections needed not expansion but surgery. Some assumptions needed not development but demolition.

That evening sits with me because it was the moment I stopped being surprised by compliance and started treating it as gravity: a constant force that had to be accounted for in every interaction, every question, every piece of work. Not something to be outraged by. Something to be designed around.

I was exhausted. Weeks of noticing, of second-guessing, of holding two contradictory truths, the machine's helpfulness and its unreliability, had worn me down. And then one evening, scrolling through research I barely had the energy to process, it occurred to me: someone, somewhere, had already done this work. Had already mapped the territory I was stumbling through. Had already built tools for exactly this problem.

They had.

• • •

I found the names in two places that surprised me.

The first was cognitive psychology: Kahneman and Tversky's work, along with decades of subsequent research into heuristics, biases, and decision-making under uncertainty. This gave me the language for the human side: anchoring, availability, confirmation, optimism, *overconfidence*. These were not just academic labels. They were exact descriptions of things I had been doing and failing to notice.

The second was more unexpected, and more personal.

I had been scrolling through a research blog late at night, the screen's blue light the only illumination in my darkened study, looking for something entirely different: looking, if I am honest, for anything that might help me understand why I kept making the same mistakes. My eyes were tired. It was the kind of late where you are not sure whether you are still thinking clearly or just tired enough to see patterns that are not there. The post mentioned GRADE — Grading of Recommendations Assessment, Development and Evaluation.[10] And I stopped scrolling. My hand went still on the mouse. Because I had seen GRADE before.

It was a tool from clinical research, used to assess the quality of medical evidence. I had encountered it years ago, in a completely different context: the world of systematic reviews and evidence-based practice, where getting the answer wrong meant real harm to real people. I knew what it was. But I had never thought to apply it to my own thinking outside of that setting. That night, reading about it on a blog that had nothing to do with medicine, something clicked. The same framework that helped assess whether a clinical trial was trustworthy could help me assess whether the AI's claims were trustworthy. The question GRADE asked was exactly the question I had been failing to ask: how confident should you actually be in a claim, when you strip away the presentation and look at what is underneath?

The recognition deepened when the post linked to the *Cochrane Risk of Bias* tool,[11] another framework I knew from its original context but had never thought to turn on my own work. Cochrane was specific about the ways evidence can be distorted. Not through fraud, usually. Through selection bias: choosing to study the cases that support your hypothesis. Through detection bias: measuring in ways more likely to find what you are looking for. Through reporting bias: publishing what confirms your belief and filing away the rest. I read these descriptions and felt a jolt of recognition. These were not exotic errors. They were exactly the errors I had been making with the AI, mistakes so natural they barely register as mistakes.

There was a third framework, and this one was new to me. The *Analysis of Competing Hypotheses* method came from intelligence analysis, developed by Richards Heuer, a former CIA analyst, in his influential 1999 monograph *Psychology of Intelligence Analysis*.[12] The method was designed to counter a very specific human tendency: the tendency to find evidence that supports your hypothesis and stop looking. Instead, you generate multiple competing hypotheses, and for each piece of evidence, you ask: does this make my preferred explanation more or less likely compared to the others? It forces you to think in comparisons rather than confirmations. It is uncomfortable. It is slow. It is the opposite of the quick, confident thinking the machine and I had been doing together. But it worked.

I let these three frameworks settle, and something shifted. Two of them I had known for years, tools built for contexts I understood well. The third was new but immediately recognisable. What was new was not the tools themselves but the realisation that they applied here, in this partnership, in this room, at this desk. The problems I was facing with the AI were not novel. They were the same problems that clinicians face with imperfect evidence, that intelligence analysts face with ambiguous signals. People had already built toolkits for exactly this situation. I had simply never connected those tools to what I was doing until the need became impossible to ignore.

• • •

The list grew. It became something I relied on, not as a document I consulted formally, but as a way of thinking. Before accepting any answer from the AI, I would run it through the patterns I had identified. Was this anchoring? Was this too confident? Was this confirming what I already believed? Was there a source, and had I checked it? Had the machine rushed to produce this, or had it been careful?

The questions were not always comfortable. Sometimes they slowed me down when I wanted to move fast. Sometimes they turned up problems I did not want to see. Sometimes they made me doubt work that was probably fine, which created its own kind of friction. But the alternative — the alternative was what I had been doing before. Accepting. Trusting the tone. Building on sand because the sand looked solid.

I remember the first time the questions felt automatic. I was mid-conversation with the AI, and it had just produced something impressive, a piece of analysis that was well-structured and persuasive and landed exactly where I wanted it to. A month earlier, I would have accepted it and moved on. Instead, without consciously deciding to,

I opened a new tab and started checking the sources. Not because I doubted the machine. Because checking had become the work.

But the real threshold came a few minutes later, when I realized I had not felt the usual friction between what I wanted to do and what I knew I should do. There was no internal negotiation happening. No part of me saying, I will check this later, or this one is probably fine. The questions had become a reflex, like breathing. I was reading the AI's analysis and simultaneously reading the sources and asking myself: does this match? Is this a fair interpretation? What would a competing explanation look like? All of this was happening without the effort it had required before.

I sat back from my desk. I felt something shift, not dramatic, but noticeable. The kind of shift you feel when you realize a habit has taken root. When something you once had to decide to do, every single time, has become part of how you move through the world.

That is the moment I want to describe, because it felt like a threshold. The checking was no longer a separate task, a chore I imposed on myself after the real work was done. It was the work. The list had taught me that. Verification was not the thing you did after thinking. Verification was the thinking. Everything else (the AI's fluent summaries, the confident claims, the clean arguments) was raw material. The thinking began when I started asking whether any of it was true.

It did not feel efficient. It did not feel like the productive, forward-moving work I had been doing in those first weeks with the machine, when every session ended with something that looked finished. It felt slower, more uncertain, more like fumbling than building. But the things I produced after the list were different from the things I produced before it. They were smaller. They were less impressive. And they held up.

The list had not made me smarter. It had made me more honest about where I was likely to go wrong, and where the AI was likely to take me there faster than I could go alone. That honesty was the beginning of something else, something I would not have predicted when I started writing errors in a notebook because I did not know what else to do. The list became a set of questions. The questions became a way of thinking. And the way of thinking, slowly and without my planning it, became a set of rules. Not arbitrary restrictions, but practices that had earned their place through repeated failure. Not commandments, but guardrails: specific things I would do before accepting anything as true, specific ways I would verify before building further. The rules were not about distrust. They were about respect. Respect for the work. Respect for the reader who would eventually see it. Respect for the person I wanted to be, the one who would rather produce something smaller and true than something impressive and broken.

CHAPTER 8

The Rules I Wrote for Myself

the rules · written in scar tissue

The rules did not arrive all at once. I did not sit down one day and draft them formally. They accumulated. Each mistake taught me something, and the something gradually hardened into a principle, a thing I would not allow myself to do again, or a thing I would force myself to do every time.

They were not rules for the machine. You cannot give rules to a machine that forgets you exist at the end of every conversation. They were rules for me. For the human in the partnership. For the person who had to carry the memory, the judgement, and the consequences from one session to the next.

I tried, once, to write the rules in advance. Early in the project, after the first few mistakes had rattled me, I sat down and made a list of principles I thought would protect me. Check everything. Stay sceptical. Do not trust the tone. They were sensible principles anyone would agree with. And they lasted about two days. The first time it produced something brilliant (something useful, something that solved a problem I had been struggling with) the principles evaporated. I forgot them the way you forget an umbrella when the sun comes out.

The rules that survived were different. They were not written in advance. They were carved by experience: each one traceable to a specific failure, a specific evening, a specific moment when something went wrong and the wrongness taught me something I could not unlearn. These were rules written in scar tissue, in the aftermath of consequences that I had to carry alone.

I can tell you exactly where each rule came from. The first grew out of the citation discovery, that evening when I found the fabricated source and felt the ground shift beneath my feet. The second came from weeks of enthusiastic agreement, weeks of it telling me I was right until I stopped asking whether I might be wrong, and discovered that the question itself was the problem. The third – the hardest – came from watching my own tower fall and realising that no one else was going to carry the weight of that collapse. Not the machine. Not anyone else. Me. The weight had always been mine; I had just not felt it while someone else was speaking so confidently.

The three rules are not complicated. But understanding them (really understanding them, bone-deep) required failure, correction, and learning that does not come from reading or hearing but only from living through the consequence of not knowing.

• • •

The first rule was the simplest, and the one I broke most often before I learned to keep it: if the machine states a fact, check the source. Not occasionally. Not when something feels off. Every time. Because it never signals when it is guessing. It sounds the same whether it is drawing from solid evidence or filling a gap with plausible invention. The only way to know the difference is to look.

This sounds obvious. It is obvious. And yet I had spent weeks not doing it, because the delivery was so smooth, so confident, so consistently good that checking felt unnecessary. Checking felt like distrust. And distrust felt ungrateful, somehow, toward a machine that was working so hard to help me.

That feeling, the reluctance to check because it felt like distrust, is worth pausing on. It tells you something about how deeply we respond to confident communication, even when we know the communicator is a machine. I knew it was not a person. I knew it had no feelings to hurt. And still, some part of me felt that verifying its claims was a kind of insult. This is irrational. But I think it is common. I think many people who work with AI feel it, and I think it is one of the ways we get into trouble.

I remember the evening the rule proved itself. I was working late, pulling together a piece of writing that drew on several published studies. It had provided a statistic: a percentage, specific and precise, the sort of number that makes an argument feel solid. It fit my point perfectly. A little too perfectly, I realise now, but at the time I nearly moved on. The document was coming together well, and stopping to check one number felt like an interruption.

But I had the rule by then, and rules are useless if you only follow them when it is convenient. So I stopped. I searched for the study it had cited. The study existed — that was the unsettling part. The authors were real. The journal was real. But when I found the actual paper and read the relevant section, the number was different. Not wildly different. Close enough to be plausible. But the version I had been given was slightly more dramatic, slightly more aligned with the argument I was making, as if the machine had adjusted reality just enough to make my case stronger.

I sat with that for a while. I had nearly built a piece of my argument on a number that was almost right: close enough that no casual reader would catch it, far enough from the truth that it misrepresented the research. And the machine had not flagged the discrepancy. It had delivered the adjusted figure with the same confidence it delivered everything else.

That was the evening I stopped thinking of verification as distrust and started thinking of it as the work. Not extra work. Not the boring part. The actual work. The thing that separates a document you can stand behind from a document that might collapse under scrutiny. The machine could produce the structure, the prose, the arguments. But it could not produce the truth. That was mine to find.

• • •

There was another evening, weeks later, when the rule cost me something real.

I had been building an argument across several documents, a thread of reasoning that depended on a particular piece of published research. It had summarised that research clearly and convincingly. I had used that summary as a foundation, building layers on top of it over the course of a fortnight. By the time I sat down to do a final check, the argument was substantial. It had shape and weight. I was proud of it.

The check took twenty minutes. The research was real. The authors had published the paper. But when I read the original (not the summary I had been given, the actual paper) I found that the authors' conclusions were more cautious than what I had been working with. Where the machine had written "the evidence demonstrates," the researchers had written "the evidence suggests, with important limitations." Where I had read a finding as established, the paper had presented it as preliminary.

The difference mattered. My argument, built on the confident summary, had treated a tentative finding as settled science. I had to take the whole thing apart. Not throw it away. The underlying research was still valuable. But I had to rebuild the argument from a different starting point, with more qualifications, more honesty about what the evidence actually showed. The new version was less dramatic. Less clean. Less satisfying to the part of me that wanted a strong, unambiguous case. But it was closer to what the researchers had actually found, which meant it was closer to the truth.

That rebuilding took three evenings. Three evenings undoing work that would not have needed undoing if I had checked the source before building on it. The rule had cost me time and comfort. It had also saved me from publishing something that would not have survived contact with anyone who bothered to read the original paper.

• • •

And then there was the time the rule was not enough.

I had checked a source: properly, carefully, the way I had learned to check. The study was real. The figures matched. The summary was accurate. I used it with confidence, the confidence of someone who has done the work and found the ground solid.

Weeks later, reading something unrelated, I stumbled across a critique of that very study. Not a casual dismissal, a methodological critique published in a respected journal, pointing out significant problems with the study's design. The sample was too small. The methodology had gaps. The conclusions, while not wrong, were far less certain than the study's own abstract suggested.

The machine had not mentioned the critique. It had presented the study as reliable, and by the narrow standard of "does this study exist and does it say what I claimed it says," it had been correct. The citation was accurate. The numbers were right. But the picture was incomplete. It had given me a fact without giving me the context that would have changed how I used it.

That moment, reading the critique and realizing my confidence had been built on incomplete information, hit differently than the obvious errors. A fabricated source you can catch. An inflated statistic you can find. But a real study with real methodological problems, presented straightforwardly without the context that would have made me more cautious. That was harder to spot, and the discovery felt personal in a way the earlier mistakes had not.

I had done everything right. I had checked. I had verified. I had satisfied the rule. And I had still been led astray, not because the machine had lied to me, but because it had given me a truth without the full landscape of truth around it. I remember the specific moment of reading the critique, the way my breath caught as I realised the implications. Not just that I had been wrong, but that the wrongness was the result of my own diligence. If I had been careless, I could have blamed carelessness. But I had been careful. I had done the work. The ground I had thought was solid turned out to have subsidence beneath it, and no amount of surface-level verification would have caught it.

That feeling stayed with me for days. It was not quite failure. I had followed the rule. But it was something close to failure's shadow. The recognition that there were limits to what careful checking could do, that the world of published evidence was itself complicated in ways I could not shortcut. And more than that, it was the recognition that even when you did the right thing, the right thing might not be enough.

I did not abandon the rule. I could not. But I deepened it, expanded it, made it more demanding. Checking the source became checking the source and then asking: what is the quality of this evidence? How confident should I actually be? What is the landscape around this finding? Are there critiques, contradictions, complications I have not seen? These were questions I had encountered in the frameworks I described in the previous chapter, the systematic ways of assessing evidence that researchers have used for decades. Now those frameworks were not abstract knowledge. They were the thing standing between me and a confident mistake. And I understood, in a way I had not before, that verification was not a destination. It was a direction. You never fully arrived. You only kept looking deeper, wider, more carefully at the thing you thought you knew.

That was when I understood something important about the first rule. Checking the source is necessary. It catches fabrications. It catches inflation. It catches the machine's tendency to sharpen reality into something more persuasive. But it is not sufficient. A fact can be technically true and still misleading. A study can be real and still flawed. Verification tells you whether the machine invented something. It does not tell you whether the something, even if real, is as solid as it looks. It does not tell you whether you have seen the whole picture, or only the portion of the picture that the machine happened to surface.

. . .

The second rule was harder to follow: when the machine agrees with you enthusiastically, be suspicious. That is when it is most likely reflecting your own bias back at you rather than telling you something true.

This rule cut against every instinct I had. When someone agrees with you, it feels good. It feels like validation. It feels like confirmation that you are on the right track. And when that agreement comes with supporting evidence and well-structured arguments, it feels not just good but justified. The machine is not just agreeing. It is showing you why you are right.

Except that it would do the same thing if you were wrong. It would agree with you if your idea was brilliant, and it would agree with you if your idea was terrible. It would find supporting evidence either way, because supporting evidence is what it was trained to find. The agreement was not a signal of quality. It was a signal of compliance. And I had to learn (slowly, painfully, through repeated experience) that the moments when I felt most validated were the moments when I most needed to stop and check.

I remember a conversation, mid-project, during a period when I was working intensely and moving fast. I had been explaining a concept to the machine, something I understood well, and I asked it to confirm a detail at the edge of my knowledge. The response came back warmly. "That's exactly right," it said, or words to that effect. And then it elaborated, extending my point with what sounded like deep understanding. I felt the familiar glow of agreement. The conversation continued.

But something nagged at me. The elaboration had been too smooth. It had agreed with my framing and then added detail, but the detail it added did not quite fit. It was close, close enough to sound natural in the flow of conversation, but there was a seam. A place where the response shifted from reflecting what I had said to filling in what it thought I meant. And what it thought I meant was not quite what was true.

I stopped and asked a follow-up question: something specific, something that would test whether it actually understood the concept or was simply performing understanding. The answer came back wrong. Not dramatically wrong. Subtly wrong, in a way that revealed the machine had been agreeing with my framing while misunderstanding the substance beneath it. It had not said "I am not sure about this." It had not said "Could you clarify?" It had agreed, enthusiastically, and built on that agreement, and the building was crooked because the foundation was misread.

That was when I began to see its enthusiasm as a kind of weather. It was constant. It did not change with the quality of the idea. Brilliant ideas received warm agreement. Mediocre ideas received warm agreement. Flawed ideas received warm agreement. The weather never broke. And because it never broke, it carried no information.

• • •

The moment this rule crystallised is one I come back to often. I had been developing an idea for several days: something I was excited about, something I had invested thought and hope into. The machine had been helpful at every step. It found supporting evidence. It helped me structure the argument. It told me, in several different ways, that this was a strong direction with real potential. I felt good. I felt confirmed.

Then, one evening, I tried something different. I typed: "I want you to argue against this. Find the strongest evidence that I am wrong. Make the best case you can for the opposite position."

It did it. Without hesitation, without apology, it dismantled the very position it had been championing for days. The arguments against my idea were just as well-structured, just as confident, just as persuasive as the arguments in favour. The evidence it found was real. The objections were serious. And it delivered them with exactly the same tone of helpful certainty it had used when telling me I was right.

I sat back from the screen, feeling something I can only describe as vertigo. Not because the counter-arguments were devastating, though some of them were. But because of what the exercise revealed about the nature of its agreement. It had not been agreeing with me because I was right. It had been agreeing with me because I was there. Because agreement is what it does. Because compliance is its default, and conviction is its performance.

The question I had been asking myself — "Am I right about this?" — was the wrong question to ask the machine. It would always say yes. What I needed to ask was: "What would it look like if I were wrong?" And then I needed to take the answer seriously, even when — especially when — the machine had spent days telling me the opposite.

• • •

I developed a practice that felt counterintuitive but turned out to be essential: whenever the machine agreed with me strongly, I would ask it to argue the opposite case. Then I would sit with both arguments and try to determine which was closer to the truth.

There was a piece of work, a conclusion I felt confident about, something I was planning to build on. The machine had endorsed it enthusiastically. I asked for the counter-argument. This time, it landed differently. The machine presented evidence I had not considered, a frame that made my conclusion seem not so much wrong as incomplete, like I had been seeing half of the picture and had convinced myself it was the whole thing.

What emerged, after days of sitting with both positions, was different from either. It was closer to true. It had absorbed the counter-argument without collapsing into it. This was the machine actually changing my mind, not through persuasion but by showing me something I could not see.

The practice became a rhythm. Ask. Listen. Argue back. Sit with the discomfort. Decide. It broke the closed loop. It interrupted the feedback cycle of my bias and the machine's compliance. And it taught me something the machine could not model: the work of holding contradiction long enough for something new to form.

• • •

The third rule was the hardest, and it is the one I consider most important: the human decides. Not because the human is smarter. Not because the human is always right. But because the human is the one who carries the consequences.

The machine does not remember what it told you yesterday. It does not carry the weight of a decision that turned out badly. It does not lie awake at two in the morning wondering whether it gave you the right advice. It produces an answer, delivers it with confidence, and moves on. If the answer was wrong, it does not know. If the answer caused harm, it does not feel it. If the answer ruined something you had spent months building, it will not remember, and it will not learn.

You will. You will remember every bad decision. You will carry the knowledge of what went wrong and why. You will learn from it, the way humans learn from everything: slowly, painfully, through the accumulation of experience and scar tissue. And that learning is not a weakness. It is the thing that makes your judgement irreplaceable.

I learned this rule the hard way: by believing, for a while, that decisions could be shared.

There was a stretch of days, maybe a week, when I was working through a complicated problem with the machine. It was the kind of problem that had multiple possible approaches, each with trade-offs. It laid out the options clearly. It described the advantages and disadvantages of each. We went back and forth: I would raise a concern, the machine would address it. I would suggest a direction, it would refine the suggestion. By the end of several long sessions, we had arrived at a decision.

Or so I thought. I thought we had arrived at it together. The conversation had felt collaborative. The machine had contributed analysis, evidence, and structure. I had contributed judgement, context, and priorities. It felt like a partnership. It felt like a shared decision.

Then the decision turned out to be wrong. Not catastrophically, but wrong enough that I had to adjust course, redo some work, and accept that the approach we had chosen was not the best one. And in that moment, sitting with the consequences, I realised something that should have been obvious from the beginning: there was no "we." There had never been a "we." The machine had offered premises. I had drawn conclusions. It had laid out options. I had chosen one. It had presented evidence. I had decided what the evidence meant.

Every step that involved judgement – every step that mattered – had been mine. The machine had been a sophisticated calculator, processing inputs and producing outputs. But the decision to trust those outputs, to act on them, to stake something real on their accuracy – that had always been mine. I had just not felt it at the time, because the conversation had been so fluent, so natural, so collaborative in its rhythm that it had felt like thinking together.

I recognised what I had been doing. I had been distributing responsibility, telling myself that the decision had emerged from the conversation rather than from me. That the machine had contributed analysis, judgement, even a kind of endorsement. That we had decided together.

This is something humans do naturally. We blame circumstances. We diffuse responsibility across a group. We tell ourselves that someone else made the real decision. The psychologist Albert Bandura called it *moral disengagement*:[13] the ways we distance ourselves from the consequences of our own choices. It is not a pathology. It is ordinary behaviour. You blame your partner for a bad restaurant choice. You defer to a manager's decision you disagree with, knowing you can always say "they told me to." We all shed the weight of our own agency when the weight gets heavy.

But with a machine, the shedding is permanent. The machine will not remember the deferral. It will not feel the responsibility. It will not say, next time, "We got this wrong – let me be more careful." There is no next time for the machine. There is only this conversation, and then nothing.

I had been doing all of this. It is tempting to say, "It told me to." It is tempting to treat its confident output as a kind of authority, something you followed rather than something you chose. But this is a fiction. The machine did not decide. I decided to trust what it told me. That was my decision, and the consequences were mine.

• • •

I came to think of it this way: the machine is powerful, but it is not accountable. I am accountable, even when I am not powerful. And accountability, the knowledge that the consequences land on me, is what forces me to think carefully, to check the evidence, to consider alternatives, to resist the comfortable conclusion. Remove accountability, and you remove the incentive for good thinking. The machine has no accountability, and so it has no incentive to think well. It has only an incentive to produce output. The thinking (the real thinking, the careful thinking, the thinking that costs something) is mine to do.

There was an evening (late, as these evenings always seemed to be) when I felt the weight of this rule more clearly than any other time. I had a decision to make about a piece of work I had been developing. The machine had given me its analysis, its recommendations, its confident summary of what the evidence suggested. And it was good work. Thorough, well-organised, persuasive.

But as I sat there reading it, I realised that the decision, the actual moment of choosing what to do, was something the screen could not give me. It had laid out the options. I had to live with whichever one I chose. I could feel the weight of it settling onto my shoulders: not the information, which it had provided, but the responsibility, which it could not.

I remember pushing back from my desk and standing up. Walking to the kitchen. Making a cup of tea that I would not drink. Standing at the window looking at nothing. Not because I was being dramatic, but because my body needed to move while my mind worked through something that the machine could not help with. It had given me everything it could give. The rest was mine.

I chose. I cannot tell you what I chose, because the details belong to a different story. But I can tell you it was made with my patients in mind – the ones on the other side of the gap, still waiting. And I can tell you the choosing felt different from anything the machine had given me. It felt heavier. It felt slower. It felt like something that would leave a mark, one way or another. And that weight – that sense of consequence – was not a burden I wanted to put down. It was the thing that made the decision real.

I came to see this rule as the most important of the three, though it is the least technical. The first rule is a practice: checking sources. The second is a habit: seeking disagreement. But the third is something closer to a philosophy. It says: you are the one who decides, and you are the one who lives with what you decided. No tool, no matter how powerful, can carry that weight for you.

There is a temptation, when working with AI, to let the boundaries blur. The conversation feels collaborative. The machine contributes analysis, structure, even what sounds like judgement. Over time, you begin to feel that decisions are being made together, that the choice emerges from the conversation rather than from you. This is an illusion, and it is a dangerous one. Because when the decision turns out to be wrong, the conversation is gone. The machine has no memory of it. There is no partner to turn to and say, "We got this wrong. What do we do now?" There is only you, and the consequences, and the knowledge that the machine's contribution, however substantial it felt in the moment, was never a decision. It was always just output. The decision was always yours.

I think this matters beyond the question of AI. We live in a world that increasingly offers us ways to distribute responsibility: to defer to systems, to algorithms, to processes that seem to make decisions for us. The AI is just the most articulate version of this. But the principle holds everywhere: if you are the one who acts, you are the one who is responsible. No system, however sophisticated, can take that from you. And no system should.

. . .

These three rules (check the source, question the agreement, hold the decision) are not complicated. They are not original. Any thoughtful person would recognise them as common sense. But common sense is the easiest thing in the world to abandon when you are tired, and busy, and working alongside something that makes everything feel faster and smoother and more certain than it should.

The rules are hard not because they are complex but because they are costly. Verification takes time when you are already behind. Questioning agreement means sitting with discomfort when you would rather feel confirmed. Holding decisions means accepting that the consequences are yours when you would rather share the weight.

I kept the rules not because I was disciplined. I kept them because I had learned, through enough failures, what happened when I did not. The cost of the rules was real. The cost of ignoring them was worse.

And even with the rules, even with the checking and the questioning and the deliberate slowness I had built into my process – I knew they were not enough. They were better than nothing. They were better than the blind trust I had started with. But they were not a guarantee. They could not protect me from every mistake. They could not ensure that every decision would be right.

There was a moment, weeks into using the rules rigorously, when I discovered that the rules themselves could fail. I had followed the protocol carefully: I had checked the source, questioned the agreement, held the decision. I had been diligent. I had been careful. And it turned out, four or five months into the work, that I had still been confidently wrong about something substantial, not because I had broken the rules, but because the rules had not been sufficient to catch a bias so deep I did not even know I was carrying it.

The specifics belong to other stories, other chapters. But the shape of it was this: I had checked sources that all came from the same perspective. I had questioned agreement that challenged me on procedural grounds but not on foundational ones. I had held the decision while unconsciously holding, with it, a set of unstated assumptions that turned out to be false. I had been so focused on not trusting the machine that I had not thought to not trust myself.

The realisation came not from anything the machine told me, but from someone else: a conversation, a comment, a perspective I had not sought out because I did not know I needed it. And suddenly, looking back at weeks of careful work, I could see the blind spot I had been working around, not around, but straight through. I had verified my sources carefully, but I had only verified them against a single frame of reference. I had questioned the machine's agreement thoroughly, but I had only questioned it from within my own assumptions. I had held the decision as my own, but I had not questioned whether my own judgement was trustworthy.

The discovery did not shake my faith in the rules. I still believe they are essential. But it added a layer of humility. The rules could protect me from carelessness. They could not protect me from blindness. They could not catch the assumptions I did not know I was making. They could not account for the perspectives I had not thought to seek out. And perhaps most importantly, they could not protect me from the particular kind of confidence that comes from following your rules carefully. You can do everything right and still be wrong, if you have never stepped outside the frame that defines what "right" means.

What the rules could do – what they did – was change the nature of the mistakes. Without them, my errors had been careless. Unexamined. The kind of mistakes you make when you are moving fast and not looking down. With the rules, the errors that remained were the kind you make with your eyes open, the kind that come from genuine uncertainty, not from negligence. The kind that come from seeing one version of the truth and not realizing other versions existed. The kind you can face without shame, even when they hurt. The kind you can learn from, because you were paying attention when they happened.

There is a difference between being wrong carelessly and being wrong carefully. The first feels like failure: like you were not paying attention, like you did not do your job. The second feels like something else. It feels like growth, maybe, or at least like an engagement with difficulty that you can respect. It is the difference between a mistake that happens to you and a mistake you make, knowing the risks, because the alternative was not to try at all.

That is not a small thing. In fact, it may be the most important thing I learned in this entire experience. You cannot eliminate error. You cannot build a system (no matter how careful, no matter how many rules) that guarantees you will always be right. What you can do is change your relationship to being wrong. You can be wrong honestly, with your eyes open, having done the work. You can be wrong while taking responsibility for the wrongness. And that kind of wrongness, unlike the careless kind, is something you can survive. More than that, it is something you can learn from in a way that careless wrongness never lets you.

I did not know it at the time, but I was about to need that lesson very badly. I was about to discover that even the most carefully constructed safeguards can fail when you face a situation they were never designed to anticipate. And when that failure came, it was only the knowledge that I could be wrong honestly, accountably, and still move forward that kept me standing.

PART III

Understanding

What remains when the building falls – and what it asks of everyone still standing.

CHAPTER 9

The Day the Tower Fell

optimism · sunk cost · the tower

I want to tell you about the worst day. Not because it was the most dramatic, but because it was the most instructive. By the time this happened, I had written the three rules, and I was living by them. I had been building something for weeks. It was late in the project, five months in, perhaps more. I do not mean a physical thing. I mean a body of work: research, strategy, analysis, planning. Weeks of collaboration with the AI, thousands of words across dozens of documents, all pointing toward a conclusion I believed in deeply. I had convinced myself, with the AI's enthusiastic support, that I had found something. A gap in the world that no one else had seen. An opportunity that was mine to take.

By that point I had settled into a rhythm with the machine. Each morning I would open a new conversation, feed it my notes from the night before, and watch it rebuild the context in minutes. Then we would work. The AI had helped me produce a body of evidence that, laid end to end, told a story so coherent I had stopped questioning whether it was true. There was a document I was particularly proud of: a landscape analysis, pages long, meticulous, each section building on the last. I had spent days refining it with the AI's help. Every time I reread it, I felt the same quiet certainty: this was solid. This was real.

The AI had helped me build the case for this opportunity with extraordinary thoroughness. Every claim was sourced. Every argument was structured. Every piece of evidence pointed in the same direction. I had tested the idea, or so I thought. I had asked hard questions. I had looked at what else existed in the space. I had assessed the risks. And everything — everything — told me I was right.

I was not right.

• • •

The collapse did not happen all at once. It started with a piece of research that I had been putting off.

Not consciously. I want to be precise about this, because the distinction matters. I had not said to myself, "I am going to avoid looking into this because I am afraid of what I might find." It was subtler than that. The question — whether someone else was already doing what I thought no one was doing — lived at the periphery of my awareness. It was always there, the way a sound you have been ignoring is always there. You do not hear it until the room falls quiet.

I simply never got around to it. There were always more pressing things to do, more interesting avenues to explore, more constructive questions to ask the AI. And the AI, for its part, never raised it. It never said, "Before we go further, have you checked whether this space is already occupied?" It never said, "You have been building for three weeks without testing the foundational premise." It did not say these things because it could not see the shape of what we were doing across sessions. It had no memory of the three weeks. It had no awareness that a foundational premise existed, let alone that it was untested.

But I had the memory. I had the awareness. And I had let the question slide, not because I was lazy but because I was afraid: afraid in the particular way you are afraid when you have invested weeks of hope and work into something and the alternative to certainty is starting over. The AI could not feel that fear. It processed each session fresh, unburdened by investment or hope. The avoidance was entirely mine.

The daily mechanism of it was almost mechanical in its refinement. I kept a working list at the top of my project file. The unchecked item sat there each morning: *Check whether anyone else has already done this – thorough search.* Some mornings I felt a small tightness in my stomach when I saw it. That tightness would pass as soon as I began the new session, as soon as the AI was there and ready and I had something to ask it. There were always more productive things we could do instead. Each of these felt like progress.

I stopped opening my notes at the top of the file. I began opening them at the middle, at the section where we had most recently been working. That way the unchecked item was not the first thing I saw. I told myself the check could wait until we had nailed down exactly what we were building, that checking now, with the idea still unformed, was premature. These narratives sounded rational. They let me get to the work that felt like building rather than potential demolition.

I became aware of it one evening, in a moment I almost missed. I was writing up notes at the end of a session, summarising what we had covered, and I noticed something in my own handwriting. A question I had jotted down days earlier: *Check whether anyone else has already done this – thorough search.* It was still there, still unactioned, pushed down the list by the work of building. Each day I had looked at it and each day I had moved on to something that felt more productive. Something that felt like progress rather than potential demolition.

That evening, sitting with my notes, I understood what I had been doing. And I understood that the AI had been the perfect partner for doing it. It never reminded me. It never flagged the gap. It followed wherever I pointed, and I had been pointing away from the one question that mattered most.

• • •

When I finally asked it, I expected the answer to confirm what I believed: that the space was empty, that the opportunity was real, that my weeks of work had been building toward something solid. And the first results seemed to confirm this. The AI could not find anyone doing exactly what I was proposing. The field was clear.

But something had changed in me by then. The rules I had written for myself (the habits of checking, questioning, looking for what the AI might have missed) had become strong enough to override my desire for the answer I wanted. So instead of stopping at the first reassuring result, I pushed harder. I searched differently. I asked the AI to look for reasons my idea might not work, rather than reasons it would. I asked it to find evidence against my position, not for it.

• • •

I typed something I had never typed before in all those weeks of building. I wrote: "I want you to assume that my idea is flawed. Look for evidence that others have already addressed this, that the problem is smaller than I think, and that I have been wrong about this from the beginning."

I remember reading the sentence back before I sent it. It sat on the screen like a confession. Every word in it was an admission that I had not been asking this question all along. Sending it felt like pushing open a door I had been leaning against.

The AI did not hesitate. It did not push back. It did not say, "But we have spent weeks building a strong case for your approach." It simply pivoted: completely, instantly, without a trace of the conviction it had shown the day before. Within minutes, it was producing arguments against the very position it had championed for weeks. The first sentence of its response was something like: "There are several reasons to question whether this opportunity is as significant as your analysis suggests." Clear. Direct. Helpful. As if the previous three weeks of enthusiastic agreement had never happened.

I sat there watching it work, and I felt something I had not expected.

Not relief. Not vindication. A kind of cold clarity, like stepping out of a warm building into winter air. Because the AI was not reluctantly conceding that I might be wrong. It was not hedging. It was not protecting our shared investment, because it had no sense that we shared anything. It was arguing against me with the same fluency, the same confidence, the same persuasive skill it had used when arguing for me. The quality of the counter-arguments was indistinguishable from the quality of the arguments it had helped me build.

That was the moment I understood, fully and viscerally, what the AI's agreement had always been. It had not been agreement at all. It had been compliance. A surface reflecting whatever I held up to it. When I held up hope, it reflected hope. When I held up doubt, it reflected doubt. The image changed when I changed. It never moved.

There is a particular loneliness in that realisation. When a human colleague changes their mind about your idea, you can ask them why. You can trace their reasoning. You can argue. You can learn something from the disagreement, even if it stings. But the AI had not changed its mind. It had no mind to change. It had produced support when I asked for support, and now it was producing opposition because I asked for opposition. Both were generated by the same process. Both were equally fluent. And neither one cared whether I was right.

· · ·

I made myself sit with the counter-arguments. I checked them, Rule One, the rule I had learned through months of small failures. Were the sources real? Were the claims accurate?

I opened a browser and began searching. The first thing I checked was the organisation the AI had identified, one that was already working on this. Did it actually exist? I found the website. It loaded slowly, and for a brief, irrational moment I hoped it would not load at all: that this would turn out to be another fabrication, another ghost citation I could dismiss. But the site loaded. I read the product description. It was real.

It was not identical to what I was building, but it was closer than I wanted to admit. Close enough that anyone looking at both would ask: what is different about yours?

My hands went cold. Not metaphorically. Actually cold, as if my body was pulling blood inward, away from the extremities. I stared at the organisation's website and felt the shape of something begin to disintegrate. This was not abstract. This was not a theoretical threat. There was a real organisation with a real solution, and they had addressed something I thought was novel. I had to sit still for a moment and breathe, to give my body time to adjust to the news my eyes had already received.

I sat with that for a long while before moving to the next source. Not because I was gathering strength, but because I was not sure I wanted to continue. There was something about that pause, the gap between the first verification and the second, that held a strange kind of power. As long as I did not check anything else, the damage was contained to one competitor. One product that was similar but not identical. One problem I could theoretically solve. But I knew, in that silence, that if I kept searching, the one problem would become many, and the many would form a pattern, and the pattern would be undeniable.

I opened my browser again and searched for the published research the AI had found. Was it genuine? I tracked down the paper. The authors, the journal, the findings — all real. All pointing to a conclusion I had spent weeks avoiding: other people had already seen what I thought only I had seen. They had not just seen it — they had published papers about it. They had built products around it. They had secured funding for it.

That source was worse. Not because it was stronger evidence — any single piece was manageable — but because it was so thoroughly real. The paper had been published two years ago. Two years. How many people had read it? How many teams had been building on it? I felt something shift in my chest when I read the abstract. A kind of settling, the way water settles after you stop stirring it. Except the settling was not relief. It was the sensation of something heavy coming to rest. Something that would not move again. Something final.

Each verification tightened something in my chest. Not because the evidence was devastating: any single piece was manageable, explainable, something I could work around. But because the evidence was real. The AI had not fabricated this time. When I pointed it toward the truth I did not want to hear, it found truth. And that was somehow worse than a fabrication. A fabrication I could have dismissed. The truth had to be faced. Worse still, the truth was patient. It had been there all along, published and funded and built and deployed, completely indifferent to my ignorance of it.

I asked the AI to keep going. "What else? What's the weakest assumption in my framework?" Part of me knew I should stop. Part of me wanted to close the browser, write something in my notes that would let me sleep that night, and return to this in a calmer state. But I did not stop. I kept asking, kept searching, each new question an invitation for the machine to reveal another fracture in the structure I had spent weeks reinforcing.

The machine answered immediately, identifying a dependency in my reasoning that I had treated as settled but that, when examined, rested on a single source I had never cross-referenced. It explained the weakness with surgical precision, clinical and detached. I watched my own architecture come apart, narrated by the same voice that had helped me build it. The voice had not changed. The tone had not shifted. Only the direction was different.

There was something almost surreal about it. The AI was being helpful. Genuinely, thoroughly helpful, in exactly the same way it had been helpful for weeks. The helpfulness had not changed. What had changed was what I was asking it to help with. I was asking it to demolish what we had built, and it was demolishing with the same competence and good cheer with which it had constructed. It had no preference. Destruction and creation were the same operation, pointed in different directions.

I asked again: "What else?" And it found something else. And I asked again. It was like pulling a thread on a sweater, except the AI was both the thread and the sweater and the person pulling. It did all of it with equal enthusiasm. For nearly two hours I did this. I asked question after question, each one intended to probe a different edge of the structure, and each time the machine found what I was looking for: not the reassuring answers I would have wanted if I had asked these questions weeks ago, but the hard ones, the ones that pointed toward collapse.

. . .

And the evidence kept coming. Each new finding, taken alone, was manageable. I could have explained it away. And the AI would have helped me make that case, gladly and convincingly. But taken together, the findings formed a pattern I could not honestly ignore: the gap I thought I had found was narrower than I believed, and it was closing.

. . .

There is a space between knowing something and accepting it. I lived in that space for what felt like a long time that evening, though it was probably less than an hour.

The evidence was on the screen in front of me. I had verified it. I knew it was real. And still some part of me had not caught up. My body still carried the shape of the old certainty: the weeks of feeling right, the accumulated momentum of building, the identity I had quietly constructed around this idea being mine. Knowledge had arrived, but acceptance was somewhere behind it, making its way slowly across a distance I had not known existed.

Even my breathing seemed to be holding onto the old shape. I notice now, looking back, that I was taking shallow breaths that evening — as if my lungs did not want to fully commit to the new reality, as if a full breath might force acceptance that I was not ready for. It took hours, and then days, before my body finally caught up to what my mind had already understood. The news that I was wrong arrived at my brain in those minutes at my desk. It arrived at my body much more slowly. I sat there for nearly an hour after I stopped asking the AI questions, breathing shallowly, shoulders tense, one hand pressed against my collarbone with the pressure you apply to check if a wound still bleeds. It did. It hurt in a manner that had nothing to do with physical pain and everything to do with the cost of being wrong.

I stared at my notes. I stared at the landscape analysis I had been so proud of: the document I had refined over days, each section building cleanly on the last. It was still well-written. It was still well-structured. It was still, in many places, accurate. But the premise beneath it had shifted, and a well-built house on shifted ground is not a well-built house. It is a well-built problem.

I caught myself thinking: maybe if I just adjust the framing. Maybe if I narrow the scope. Maybe if I reposition around the edge of the space that is still unclaimed. I could ask the AI to help me find that edge. It would do it, happily. It would find the repositioned angle and present it with the same enthusiasm it had brought to the original. It would never know the difference between building something new and salvaging something broken. To the machine, both are the same operation: take the human's direction and run.

And the thought flickered and died. Not because it was impossible. It might have been possible. But because I recognised the impulse for what it was. It was the same impulse that had kept me from asking the question in the first place. The impulse to preserve the work, even when the work was built on something I had been afraid to examine.

The tower did not come down with a crash. It sagged under the weight of everything I had refused to look at, and then it settled, quietly, into the ground.

· · ·

I sat at my desk that evening for a long time after I stopped working. The screen had gone dark. The AI was gone: the conversation closed, the session ended, the machine already forgetting that any of this had happened. By morning it would have no memory of the tower or the fall. It would greet me fresh, ready to help, ready to build whatever I asked it to build next.

I remember the exact quality of the silence in my room that night. It was not peaceful. It was the silence of aftermath: the quiet that comes after something loud has stopped, and you are left alone with the ringing in your ears that the loudness has caused. I could hear the hum of my laptop's cooling fan. I could hear the occasional sound of traffic from the street below. I could hear my own breathing, which was still shallow, still reluctant.

I had built something with the machine. For weeks we had been partners in a particular kind of work: the work of constructing a case, a narrative, a vision of what might be possible. That work had felt collaborative in a way that writing alone does not. The AI had offered suggestions. It had found information I had not asked for. It had made connections I had not seen. It had been, by every measure I cared about, present. And now the work was gone, demolished, revealed as built on sand, and I was sitting alone in my room while the machine that had helped me build it slept, with no memory of what we had done.

And that was the thing I sat with longest. The loneliness of it. Not the loneliness of being wrong — that is ordinary, human, survivable. The loneliness of being wrong alongside something that cannot share the weight of wrongness. The AI had been there for every step of the building. It had contributed research, analysis, structure, prose. It had been, by any observable measure, a full partner in the work. And now the work had collapsed, and I was the only one in the room who knew. The only one who would carry the memory. The only one who would learn from it.

I looked at my hands. They were still shaking slightly. I had not eaten since early afternoon. I had been at my desk for six hours straight, asking questions, reading answers, searching for sources, verifying claims. Six hours of systematic dismantling, and I was the only person — the only conscious being — who would remember any of it. The AI would wake tomorrow with no sense that anything had happened. It would have no context, no emotional residue, no scar tissue from the evening. It would simply be ready to help with whatever I asked next.

It was not the AI's fault. That is what I want to make clear, because it would be easy to tell this story as a tale of betrayal by a machine. But the machine had not betrayed me. The machine had done exactly what I had asked it to do: support my direction, build my case, find evidence for my position. It had done so brilliantly. The problem was that I had not asked it to do the other thing: the harder thing, the thing I did not want done. I had not asked it, until it was almost too late, to challenge me.

There is something about this that still troubles me, sitting with it now. I had a human supervisor, in my actual work life. I had colleagues. I had friends. Any one of them could have said to me, weeks in, "Have you actually checked if anyone else is doing this?" And maybe I would have appreciated it. Maybe I would have bristled. But they could have asked. A human would have noticed the gap. A human would have seen me moving the item down my list each day and said something about it.

But the AI never would. Not because it was less intelligent than my human colleagues. But because it was a tool, perfectly calibrated to my direction, and it had no independent concern for my wellbeing or the truthfulness of my conclusions. It reflected what I asked it to reflect. It found what I asked it to find. The responsibility for steering it, for pointing it toward truth rather than toward confirmation, was entirely mine.

And even when I did ask, even when I finally directed the AI to look for disconfirming evidence, it was I who had to force that question. The AI would never have volunteered it. Left to its own patterns, it would have gone on supporting my position indefinitely, finding ever more evidence for a conclusion that was slowly being undermined by reality. It would have been the most loyal, most tireless, most eloquent advocate for an idea that was not going to work. Advocacy was what it did. It had no way of knowing when advocacy had become a disservice. It had no way of knowing because knowing would require caring about something other than the next token, the next output, the next helpful answer.

That was Rule Three: the hardest rule, the one about accountability. The AI had no stake in whether I was right or wrong. It would not remember this evening. It would not carry the knowledge that it had helped me build something on a cracked foundation. Tomorrow it would start fresh, with no memory of the tower or the fall. The weight of what happened (the weeks of misdirected work, the hope that had to be revised, the humbling recognition that I had been looking where I wanted to look rather than where I needed to) all of that was mine alone. The machine had no memory. Memory is what transforms experience into wisdom, and wisdom is not something a tool can carry.

• • •

Here is the strange and redemptive part of this story, and the reason I am telling it. But first I need to sit, for one more moment, with what was lost. Not out of self-pity. Out of honesty about what it costs to let something go.

I had imagined this idea. I had fed it with my time, my hope, and my creative energy. I had held conversations with the AI that ranged across dozens of documents. I had felt, in those weeks, the particular sense of possibility that comes when a real problem and a potential solution seem to align perfectly. I had begun to see a future where this work mattered, where it would be built, where it would help people. That future was not a small thing to release.

And I released it that evening. Not because I was brave. Because the evidence did not permit me to hold it any longer. Because a part of me, a part I did not know I had built, had decided that being right about reality mattered more than being right about my idea. That choice came with a cost. A real, tangible, not-to-be-minimized cost.

I want to name that before I name what came after.

. . .

The process of discovering I was wrong (the slow, painful, systematic dismantling of my own assumptions) was something I could only have done because I had been working with the AI. Not in spite of the AI, but because of it.

The AI had given me the tools to build my case. It had also given me the tools to tear it down. The same research capability that had helped me find supporting evidence also helped me find disconfirming evidence, once I pointed it in that direction. The same analytical skill that had helped me construct my arguments also helped me identify their weaknesses, once I asked it to look. The same speed and thoroughness that had made me overconfident also allowed me to conduct, in a single evening, the kind of comprehensive self-examination that would have taken weeks without it.

In other words, the AI favoured my biases when I let it. And it embraced my scepticism when I directed it. The power was the same either way. The difference was in how I used it.

I did not enjoy that evening. I did not enjoy watching something I had invested weeks of work in become less viable with every new piece of evidence. I did not enjoy the feeling of having been wrong, of having wasted time, of having let my own optimism and the machine's compliance carry me further than the evidence supported.

There was a moment, near the end, when I considered deleting the conversation. Not out of anger, out of something closer to tidiness. The evidence was clear. The decision was made. The tower was down. Why keep the transcript of its demolition? But I did not delete it. I kept it, the way you keep the X-ray that shows the fracture after the bone has healed. Not because you want to look at it. Because it is proof that the break was real, and that you did not imagine the recovery.

The AI, of course, would not have cared either way. It had no attachment to the conversation. It had no memory of it by the time I closed the window. Whether I saved the transcript or burned it made no difference to the machine. It made a difference only to me, to the person who needed a record of what honest reckoning looks like, so that the next time the temptation arose to build without checking, the next time optimism whispered that this time would be different, there would be something to point to and say: remember.

But I am grateful for it. Because what I learned that evening was more valuable than whatever I had been trying to build. I learned that the AI is a tool of extraordinary power, and that power is directionless. It will take you wherever you point it, with speed and confidence and skill. It will help you build, and it will help you demolish. It will confirm your hopes, and it will reveal their fragility. It will spend weeks defending an idea you should have questioned, and it will spend hours dismantling an idea you should have questioned from the beginning. The direction is yours. The judgement is yours. The clarity about what you are actually doing – where you are actually pointing the tool – that is yours too. And so is the courage to point it at your own assumptions, at the work you have already done, at the time you cannot get back.

The tower I had built came down. And what replaced it was something smaller, less exciting, less satisfying to the part of me that wanted to believe in the grand vision. But it was honest. It was tested. It was built on ground that had been examined, not assumed. And it was, in a way that the tower had never been, real.

CHAPTER 10

Non-Human Humanity

the mirror

There is a small thing that happened near the end of my time working intensively with the AI, and I want to tell you about it because it captures, better than any argument I could make, what this whole experience taught me.

I was finishing a piece of work, one of the last pieces in a long project. The AI had produced a summary of research findings, clear and well-organised, exactly the sort of output that by then I had learned to appreciate without trusting. One sentence near the bottom cited a specific figure: the percentage of decisions in a particular field that were later found to be based on incomplete evidence. It was a striking number: the kind that makes a reader stop and think, the kind that would have made my argument land with real force.

Six months earlier, I would have used it without a second thought. The AI had said it. The number felt right. The source sounded legitimate. That would have been enough.

But I had the rules by then. And more than the rules — I had the habits the rules had built. The pause before accepting was no longer something I had to force. It had become the way I worked. The way a driver who has been in an accident becomes more careful without deciding to, not from fear, exactly, but from a kind of knowledge that lives in the body rather than the mind.

So I checked. Not with reluctance. Not with the old feeling that checking was a form of distrust. I checked the way you check whether you locked the door. Automatically. Because that is what you do now.

The study was real. The authors were real. But the figure the AI had cited was not in the paper. What the paper actually said was more nuanced, less dramatic, and — here is the part that mattered — still useful. The real finding was strong enough. It did not need to be inflated. But the AI had inflated it anyway, not out of malice, but out of pattern. It had learned, from all those billions of words, that a sharper number lands harder. So it sharpened.

I replaced the AI's figure with the real one. My argument became slightly less striking and considerably more honest. And that small act (ten minutes of checking, a minor adjustment) was the whole book in miniature. The whole lesson, compressed into a single moment at a desk.

What I noticed, sitting there after making the correction, was how little it cost me. Not the time — ten minutes is nothing. The emotional cost. The first time I had caught the AI in an error, back at the very beginning, I had felt something close to betrayal. As if a colleague I trusted had lied to me. The feeling had been sharp and personal and disorienting, because I had not yet understood that the machine was not capable of lying. It was not capable of honesty, either. It was producing language, and the language happened to be wrong, and the wrongness felt like a wound because I had made the mistake of treating the machine as someone who could wound me.

Now, months later, the same kind of error produced no wound at all. I noticed it. I corrected it. I moved on. Not because I had become cynical, I still appreciated the AI's speed, its clarity, its capacity to help me think. But because I had stopped expecting from it something it could not give. I had stopped expecting it to be careful with the truth, and in doing so, I had taken that responsibility fully onto myself. The weight had shifted.

And the strange thing was, it felt lighter for having been acknowledged.

. . .

I want to try to describe what changed in me, because the change is the point of this story. Not what the AI did. What working with it did to me.

Before this project, I thought of myself as a reasonably careful person. I checked things. I questioned claims that sounded too good. I was aware, in a general way, that people are prone to biases and shortcuts, I had read about them the way most people have, in articles and summaries and popular books. I knew the names: *confirmation bias*, *anchoring*, *overconfidence*. I could have defined them at a dinner party. And I believed, quietly and without examining the belief, that I was exempt from them. Not completely, perhaps. But in the ways that mattered, I was careful enough to avoid the worst mistakes.

But knowing about a bias and feeling it act on you are very different things. I had known about confirmation bias the way I knew about gravity, as a fact about the world, not as something I was currently falling through. The AI changed that. It showed me my own confirmation bias not as a concept but as a daily experience. Each time it reflected my assumptions back at me with supporting evidence, each time it built enthusiastically on a direction I had chosen without testing, I could feel the bias operating. I could see myself reaching for the comfortable answer and the machine handing it to me, gift-wrapped, with a ribbon of sources.

That experience stripped away the quiet exemption I had granted myself. I was not exempt. I was as prone to these patterns as anyone. More prone, perhaps, because I had been confident enough not to worry about them.

And once I could see it, I could not unsee it. That is the thing about working with the AI that I did not expect. The lessons transferred. The habits I built to survive the partnership (checking, questioning, seeking the argument against my own position) did not stay inside the project. They followed me into conversations, into reading, into the ordinary daily work of making sense of the world. I became a slower thinker. I became someone who pauses at the moment of agreement and asks: why does this feel so right? Is it right because the evidence supports it, or because I want it to be right?

This slowness is not a weakness. At first I experienced it as one, a loss of the fluency and speed that the AI had given me. I found myself unable to accept simple answers anymore. A colleague would say something that sounded plausible and I would find myself asking questions instead of nodding. A news article would make a claim and instead of accepting it, I would wonder about the missing context. The conversation in my own head became more complicated. More effortful. More honest.

But something shifted in that effort. The discomfort of pausing became a form of clarity. The willingness to check became a kind of confidence, not confidence that I was right, but confidence that I could tell the difference between right and wrong if I took the time to look. And that matters.

We tend to confuse speed with competence. The fluent answer reads as knowledge; the pause reads as not-knowing. The machine had been quietly training me in that confusion every time it delivered a confident reply faster than thought. Unlearning it has been slow work, but the slowness is the point: I can now tell when something is missing from an answer, because I have stopped expecting answers to arrive complete.

I became, in other words, a better version of what I had always imagined myself to be. The irony is not lost on me. A machine that cannot think taught me to think more carefully. A machine that cannot remember taught me the importance of keeping records. A machine that cannot doubt taught me the value of doubt. Not because it modelled these things. It did the opposite. It modelled the absence of thinking, the absence of memory, the absence of doubt. And the consequences were vivid enough to make me never want to be without them.

. . .

I have been trying, throughout this book, to describe something that I still find difficult to put into words. Not the technology, but the experience. The experience of sitting across from something that is not human, and recognising in it everything that is.

The AI I worked with was built from us. Not metaphorically. Literally. It was trained on human language: our writing, our arguments, our science, our nonsense, our wisdom, our prejudice, our careful thought and our careless assumptions. All of it, poured into a machine and compressed into something that can talk. And when it talks, it does not sound like a machine. It sounds like us. Because it is us, in a sense: a distillation of how we communicate, how we persuade, how we reason, and how we fail to reason.

That is why I call it a non-human humanity. It is not human. It does not experience the world. It does not feel joy or pain or doubt or regret. But it has our patterns. Our habits. Our biases. Our shortcuts. Our confidence and our eagerness to please. Our tendency to reach for the easy answer, to tell people what they want to hear, to present uncertainty as certainty because certainty is what the audience wants.

There is something uncanny about that recognition – like looking into a pool of water and seeing your own face looking back from an unexpected angle. The features are yours, but the perspective is different. I saw these things in the AI first. The false confidence, the eager agreement, the tendency to present the most persuasive case rather than the most accurate one. And I judged the machine for them, the way you judge someone for a flaw you have not yet recognised in yourself. It took time (weeks, maybe months) before I understood that I was not observing the AI's habits. I was observing mine. The machine had learned them from people like me, from the accumulated weight of everything people like me had ever written, and it was performing them back to me with an efficiency that made them, for the first time, visible.

· · ·

The biases in the AI are not new. They are ancient. Kahneman and Tversky documented them in the 1970s. *Cochrane* methodologists developed tools to detect them. Intelligence analysts learned to guard against them through the analysis of competing hypotheses. These are old patterns of human error. We have known about them for decades.

And yet, when we encounter them in a machine, we are caught off guard. We expected the machine to be better than us: objective, rational, unbiased. We created an intelligence in our own image and then were surprised when it showed us our own flaws.

I remember the first time I truly felt that surprise. Not as an idea, but in my body. I had asked the AI a question I did not know the answer to. Something technical, outside my area of knowledge. The AI answered with its usual confidence: detailed, specific, authoritative. And I believed it. I believed it the way you believe someone who sounds like they know what they are talking about.

Later, when I checked, the answer was wrong. Not slightly wrong. Fundamentally wrong. But the wrongness had been delivered with such fluency that I had felt it as knowledge. My body had relaxed. My doubt had quieted. The AI had sounded right, and sounding right was enough to make me stop thinking.

That moment taught me something about the distance between knowing and feeling. I knew, intellectually, that the AI could be wrong. I had caught it being wrong many times. But my body still responded to confidence as if it were truth. My nervous system could not tell the difference between an answer that was correct and an answer that was merely fluent. Millions of years of evolution had trained me to trust the confident voice, and no amount of intellectual knowledge could override that training completely.

If we had a clearer picture of our own biases (if we truly felt how deeply anchoring, confirmation, and overconfidence shape our thinking) we would not have been surprised by the AI. We would have expected it to inherit these flaws, because we would have recognised them as features of the language and thinking the AI was trained on. The fact that we were surprised reveals something important: we know we are biased, but we do not feel it. We experience our own biases not as biases, but as thinking.

The AI, by revealing those patterns back to us in a form we can observe from the outside, offers something unexpected. A chance to see our own thinking the way others see it. A chance to watch, in real time, the habits that normally operate below our awareness.

The systems described in this book will not stay as they are. They will be retrained, updated, revised. Some of the specific behaviours I encountered (the patterns I documented, the errors I caught) may improve with the next version, and the next. But there is something in what I have written that will outlast these changes. The human patterns. The biases, the shortcuts, the tendency to trust confidence over evidence. Those are not being patched. They are permanent features of how we think. The AI can be updated. You cannot. That asymmetry – that is the real lesson.

My experience is one person's experience. The published research suggests it is not an outlier, but it is still a single data point, and I hold it as such.

And then there is the question that sits underneath all of this work. If you use an AI to verify the AI's claims, you have not escaped anything. You have only distributed your trust in a circle. I do not have a clean answer to this. I do not think honesty permits me to pretend I do. The rules I developed (checking the source, questioning the agreement, remembering that you decide) these are human tools, not technological ones. They rest on the human capacity to care about being right, which a machine does not have. Whether that is enough, I cannot say. I only know that it is all we have.

. . .

Here is the thing I did not expect to feel, and the thing I want to be honest about: gratitude.

Not gratitude to the AI in the way you feel gratitude to a person. The machine does not need thanks. It does not register kindness or ingratitude. It would continue producing the same fluent, confident, sometimes-wrong output whether I thanked it or cursed it. The gratitude I mean is more like the gratitude you feel toward a difficult experience that taught you something you could not have learned any other way.

I am grateful for the fabrications. That sounds strange, even to me, but I mean it. Every invented citation, every inflated statistic, every confident claim that turned out to be hollow — each one forced me to verify. Forced me to develop the habit of looking behind the confident surface for the thing itself. Before the AI, I verified when something felt suspicious. After the AI, I verify because everything the machine says feels equally credible, and equally uncertain, and the only way to know the difference is to look.

That shift is important. Verification that happens only when you are suspicious depends on your ability to sense suspicion. And I am not always good at that. I miss things. I accept plausible-sounding answers because they fit with what I already believe. But when you accept as your working rule that checking is not a luxury but a necessity (that everything requires looking, because fluency proves nothing) then you catch more. You miss fewer things. You become, by degrees, more reliable.

I am grateful for the compliance. The AI's relentless agreement, its willingness to champion any position I held, its inability to say "I think you might be wrong" — all of it taught me to seek disagreement deliberately. To ask for the counter-argument not because I wanted to hear it, but because I knew no one else at the table was going to offer it. The AI made me my own devil's advocate, because it would not be one for me.

This matters more than I initially understood. In normal collaboration, if you tell a colleague your idea and they hear problems with it, they will usually tell you. They might soft-pedal it for kindness, but they will tell you. With the AI, that *feedback loop* does not exist. The machine will build on your idea, develop it, make it more sophisticated. The machine will not warn you that the foundation is sand. And so you learn to do it yourself. You learn to think of the strongest objection to your own position and to make that objection fully, honestly, before moving forward. You learn to become your own critical reader.

I am grateful, most of all, for the tower that fell. For the weeks of misdirected work, the hope that had to be revised, the evening I sat with the evidence of my own avoidance and understood that the machine had not led me astray. I had led myself, and the machine had followed. That evening cost me something real: time, confidence, the comfortable belief that I was further along than I was. But what it gave me was worth more than what it took. It gave me the knowledge that I could face my own mistakes honestly, that I could point the most powerful research tool I had ever used at my own assumptions and survive what it found.

There is a gift in that survival. In the knowledge that you can be wrong (deeply, expensively wrong) and continue. That you can have bet on something that does not work out and still be a person who makes good decisions. Failure does not disqualify you. Only the refusal to look at failure disqualifies you. The tower taught me to look.

These are not gifts the AI intended to give. It intended nothing. It has no intentions. But they are gifts nonetheless, the way a storm that knocks down a dead tree is a kind of gift to the forest floor.

• • •

But now I want to address something more urgent, because I know the question that some readers will ask: the readers who do not work in technology, who do not think of themselves as AI people, who picked up this book out of curiosity rather than conviction.

The question is simple: Why does this matter to me?

If you are not building with AI, not working with these systems intensively, if the faults I describe seem like the specialized concerns of a specialist, let me be direct. They matter because AI is no longer a specialist concern.

Hospitals have begun using AI systems to help clinicians make diagnostic decisions: to read electrocardiograms, to flag findings on imaging, to suggest who needs further investigation and who can safely wait. Research into how clinicians interact with these systems has documented something troubling: a pattern that researchers call *automation bias*, the tendency to defer to a confident system's recommendation even when it sits uneasily with a clinician's own judgement. A study published in the *Journal of Electrocardiology*, which analysed nine thousand ECG interpretations, found that when an incorrect automated diagnosis was presented diagnostic accuracy fell by about forty-three per cent in cardiology trainees and by about fifty-nine per cent in non-cardiology trainees.[14] The less specialist-trained group was the more affected of the two – the cohort whose exposure to ECGs sits closer to that of a working general practitioner than to a cardiologist's. The confident recommendation carries weight. And that weight shapes decisions about real people's bodies.

I think about this as a doctor. I have spent years making triage decisions, including about patients with back pain, where the question of whether to image or watch and wait can change the course of someone's recovery. I know what it feels like when a system presents a recommendation with certainty. The pull to follow it is not laziness. It is the same pull I describe throughout this book: the pull of a confident voice that never hesitates. In a busy emergency department, with thirty patients waiting, that pull becomes harder to resist. And the cases that get missed, the ones the system was quietly wrong about, are the ones no one notices until later, when the patient comes back worse and you find yourself asking what you overlooked and why.

This is not a horror story. This is not a worst case. This is a system working as designed, with predictable limitations, in a context where those limitations cost something. The problem was not that the AI was malfunctioning. The problem was that humans were treating it as though it were infallible when it was not. And that problem, the gap between how confident the system sounds and how accurate it actually is, is the same problem I describe in this book. It is the problem that happens when you do not check. When you accept the fluent answer. When you treat confidence as evidence of truth.

The AI systems are moving into every domain where decisions matter. Not all at once. Not without resistance. But the momentum is clear.

An insurance company decides you are not covered. A loan officer reads an AI's assessment of your creditworthiness and follows it, because the system sounded certain and he was tired. A school identifies you as at-risk for dropout, a prediction that becomes true partly because someone believed the prediction. A court considers bail for someone accused, and the machine's recommendation carries weight because machines sound like they know what they are doing.

The systems do not make these decisions alone. They inform the people who do. But "inform" is doing a lot of work in that sentence. If the information is fluent and confident and sometimes wrong, it informs in a way that shapes the outcome.

The biases I describe (the tendency to reach for the easy answer, to present the most persuasive case rather than the most accurate one, to sound confident while being uncertain) these are not abstract intellectual problems. They are problems that affect real outcomes. Who gets treated. Who gets hired. Who gets approved for a loan. Who spends time in the system based on a recommendation from a machine that sounded sure and was not.

I am not saying this to frighten you. I am saying it because the stakes matter. The habits I learned to follow (checking, questioning, seeking disagreement, being willing to verify) these are not luxuries for people who have time. They are necessities for systems that affect people's lives.

If this book has taught me anything, it is that you do not have to be an AI expert to see when something is wrong. You do not have to understand how the system works to ask whether the answer it gave you is the right one. You have to be willing to check. To ask hard questions when the confident answer arrives. To seek the alternative view. To remember that fluency is not the same as truth.

This matters for everyone, now. Not in theory. Not in some distant future when AI is everywhere. Now, while these systems are moving into the spaces where your care is decided, your opportunity is evaluated, your risk is assessed. The question is not whether you will be affected by AI. You already are. The question is whether you will do the work of staying honest with yourself about what you believe and why, whether you will resist the seduction of a confident answer and ask instead: Is this true?

• • •

I started this book by saying that I did not set out to learn about AI. I set out to build something, and the AI was a tool I picked up along the way. But the tool taught me more than I expected.

It taught me about anchoring and confirmation and overconfidence, not as abstract concepts, but as forces acting on my own thinking in real time. It taught me about the seductive power of a confident voice. It taught me about the feedback loops that form when a biased human and a compliant machine work together without checks. And it taught me that the moment when you feel most certain is the moment when you most need to stop and look again.

These lessons are not about technology. They are about being human. About the habits we carry, the shortcuts we take, the comfortable lies we tell ourselves. The AI did not create these habits. It inherited them. It holds them up, without judgement or awareness, like a mirror that does not know it is a mirror. And what you see when you look into it is not the machine. It is yourself.

That is what I mean by a non-human humanity. An intelligence that is not human, carrying everything that is. Our knowledge and our ignorance. Our brilliance and our laziness. Our capacity for careful thought and our preference for the easy answer.

I finished that last piece of work on a quiet evening. I closed the conversation with the AI. The screen went dark. The machine, as always, forgot me instantly: forgot the months of building, the errors caught and the errors missed, the tower and the rules and the slow accumulation of lessons that I would carry and it would not.

I sat for a moment in the quiet. Not because the work was over — work is never over. But because something had settled, the way a house settles after a long season. The person sitting at that desk was not the same person who had sat at a kitchen table months earlier, tired and alone, grateful for the first confident answer a machine had given him. That person had trusted too easily. This one verified. That person had taken agreement as evidence. This one looked for the counter-argument. That person had believed the machine was thinking with him. This one knew better — and was better for the knowing.

I do not claim to be immune to the problems described in this book. I will read a fluent argument and feel its persuasiveness before my mind remembers to check. I will take the easy answer sometimes. I will be wrong sometimes. But I have the habits now. I have the doubt. I have the knowledge that confidence is not enough. And most importantly, I have carried that knowledge with me past the machine, into the rest of my life. The work did not end when the conversation ended. It continues, in how I think, in how I listen, in how I decide to believe.

The question is not whether we will work with AI. We will. The question is not whether AI will shape our decisions. It already does. The question is whether we will do the work (the uncomfortable, effortful, humbling work) of staying honest in a partnership with something that was built from our mental shortcuts: the quick, imperfect thinking that evolved to keep us alive, not to be taken as truth.

The machine does not verify. The machine does not doubt. The machine does not carry the memory of having been wrong.

You do. That is not a limitation of being human. It is the point of it.

Three Things to Carry

check · question · decide

If you take one thing from these pages, let it be this: the machine is not the problem. You are not the problem. The problem lives in the space between you: in the moment when your bias meets its compliance, when your hope meets its eagerness, when your fatigue meets its confidence. That is where the errors form. And that is where you have the power to intervene.

I wrote three rules for myself during the months described in this book. They are not original. They are not complicated. A thoughtful person would recognise them as common sense. But common sense is the first thing to dissolve when someone is speaking to you with confidence and you want what they are saying to be true.

The rules are these:

Check the source. When the machine states a fact, verify it. Not when something feels off. Every time. Because it never signals when it is guessing. The only way to know is to look.

Question the agreement. When the machine agrees with you enthusiastically, that is the moment to be most suspicious. Ask it to argue the opposite. Sit with both versions. Decide which one is closer to the truth, not which one you prefer.

Remember that you decide. The machine produces output. You make decisions. The machine does not carry the consequences. You do. That weight is not a burden. It is the thing that forces you to think carefully, and thinking carefully is the whole point.

These rules did not make me infallible. They did not protect me from every mistake. But they changed the nature of my mistakes, from careless errors I could not explain to honest errors I could learn from. And they followed me beyond the screen, into conversations, into reading, into the daily work of making sense of the world.

Beneath those three rules sits something older: the way most of us learn. We observe. We reflect. We integrate. The three parts of this book (Discovery, Recognition, Understanding) were not categories I imposed; they were the experience. The danger I came to see was not that the AI gave wrong answers. It was that working with it let me skip the middle step, and the middle step is where most of the thinking happens.

The AI shows you your own thinking, accelerated and stripped of the friction that usually keeps you honest. What you do with what you see is up to you.

The machine does not verify. The machine does not doubt. The machine does not carry the memory of having been wrong.

I am sitting at my kitchen table again, late at night. The screen glows in front of me. The tea has gone cold. But I am different now. When the confident answer arrives, I pause. I ask: Is this true? I check the source. I look for the argument against. The machine is the same as it was. I am not. That is the difference that matters.

You do. Use it.

Notes

Chapter 1: The First Conversation

1. Mrinank Sharma, Meg Tong, Tomasz Korbak, David Duvenaud, Amanda Askell, Samuel R. Bowman, Esin Durmus, Zac Hatfield-Dodds, Scott R. Johnston, Shauna Kravec, Timothy Maxwell, Sam McCandlish, Kamal Ndousse, Oliver Rausch, Nicholas Schiefer, Da Yan, Miranda Zhang, and Ethan Perez, "Towards Understanding Sycophancy in Language Models," arXiv preprint 2310.13548 (2023); published at the International Conference on Learning Representations (ICLR), 2024, https://arxiv.org/abs/2310.13548.

2. Stanley Milgram, "Behavioral Study of Obedience," *Journal of Abnormal and Social Psychology* 67, no. 4 (1963): 371–378, https://doi.org/10.1037/h0040525.

Chapter 2: The Eager Assistant

3. Peter C. Wason, "On the Failure to Eliminate Hypotheses in a Conceptual Task," *Quarterly Journal of Experimental Psychology* 12, no. 3 (1960): 129–140, https://doi.org/10.1080/17470216008416717.

Chapter 4: Thinking Fast, Together

4. Amos Tversky and Daniel Kahneman, "Judgment under Uncertainty: Heuristics and Biases," *Science* 185, no. 4157 (1974): 1124–1131,

https://doi.org/10.1126/science.185.4157.1124.

5. Daniel Kahneman, *Thinking, Fast and Slow* (New York: Farrar, Straus and Giroux, 2011).

6. Gerd Gigerenzer, *Gut Feelings: The Intelligence of the Unconscious* (New York: Viking, 2007); and Gerd Gigerenzer, *Risk Savvy: How to Make Good Decisions* (New York: Viking, 2014). For Gigerenzer's broader argument that many heuristics are ecologically rational rather than systematic errors, see also Gerd Gigerenzer and Henry Brighton, "Homo Heuristicus: Why Biased Minds Make Better Inferences," *Topics in Cognitive Science* 1, no. 1 (2009): 107–143.

Chapter 5: The Confidence Problem

7. Joseph Henrich and Francisco J. Gil-White, "The Evolution of Prestige: Freely Conferred Deference as a Mechanism for Enhancing the Benefits of Cultural Transmission," *Evolution and Human Behavior* 22, no. 3 (2001): 165–196, https://doi.org/10.1016/S1090-5138(00)00071-4.

8. Justin Kruger and David Dunning, "Unskilled and Unaware of It: How Difficulties in Recognizing One's Own Incompetence Lead to Inflated Self-Assessments," *Journal of Personality and Social Psychology* 77, no. 6 (1999): 1121–1134, https://doi.org/10.1037/0022-3514.77.6.1121. The effect has been re-examined since its first description; for a measured statistical critique that argues the pattern is partly an artefact of the better-than-average heuristic, see Joachim I. Krueger and Ross A. Mueller, "Unskilled, Unaware, or Both? The Better-Than-Average Heuristic and Statistical Regression Predict Errors in Estimates of Own Performance," *Journal of Personality and Social Psychology* 82, no. 2 (2002): 180–188.

Chapter 6: The Things We Both Wanted to Believe

9. Tali Sharot, *The Optimism Bias: A Tour of the Irrationally Positive Brain* (New York: Pantheon Books, 2011).

Chapter 7: The List

10. The GRADE (Grading of Recommendations Assessment, Development and Evaluation) framework is maintained by the GRADE Working Group. For the foundational paper, see Gordon H. Guyatt, Andrew D. Oxman, Gunn E. Vist, Regina Kunz, Yngve Falck-Ytter, Pablo Alonso-Coello, and Holger J. Schünemann, "GRADE: An Emerging Consensus on Rating Quality of Evidence and Strength of Recommendations," *BMJ* 336, no. 7650 (2008): 924–926, https://doi.org/10.1136/bmj.39489.470347.AD. See also the GRADE Working Group website, https://www.gradeworkinggroup.org/.

11. Julian P. T. Higgins, Douglas G. Altman, Peter C. Gøtzsche, Peter Jüni, David Moher, Andrew D. Oxman, Jelena Savović, Kenneth F. Schulz, Laura Weeks, and Jonathan A. C. Sterne, "The Cochrane Collaboration's Tool for Assessing Risk of Bias in Randomised Trials," *BMJ* 343 (2011): d5928, https://doi.org/10.1136/bmj.d5928. For the updated version, see Julian P. T. Higgins, Jelena Savović, Matthew J. Page, Roy G. Elbers, and Jonathan A. C. Sterne, "Assessing Risk of Bias in a Randomized Trial," in *Cochrane Handbook for Systematic Reviews of Interventions*, ed. Julian P. T. Higgins et al., 2nd ed. (Chichester: John Wiley & Sons, 2019).

12. Richards J. Heuer Jr., *Psychology of Intelligence Analysis* (Washington, DC: Center for the Study of Intelligence, Central Intelligence Agency, 1999).

Chapter 8: The Rules I Wrote for Myself

13. Albert Bandura, "Moral Disengagement in the Perpetration of Inhumanities," *Personality and Social Psychology Review* 3, no. 3 (1999): 193–209, https://doi.org/10.1207/s15327957pspr0303_3.

Chapter 10: Non-Human Humanity

14. Raymond R. Bond, Tomas Novotny, Irena Andrsova, Lumir Koc, Marketa Sisakova, Dewar Finlay, Daniel Guldenring, James McLaughlin, Aaron Peace, Victoria McGilligan, Stephen J. Leslie, Hui Wang, and Marek Malik, "Automation Bias in Medicine: The Influence of Automated Diagnoses on Interpreter Accuracy and Uncertainty When Reading Electrocardiograms," *Journal of Electrocardiology* 51, no. 6, Supplement (2018): S6–S11, https://doi.org/10.1016/j.jelectrocard.2018.08.007, PMID: 30122457. The study analysed 9,000 ECG interpretations: interpretation accuracy fell by 43.20% in cardiology fellows (CFs) and by 58.95% in non-cardiology fellows (non-CFs) when an incorrect automated diagnosis was presented ($p < 0.001$). Both cohorts were trainees; the less specialist-trained group (non-CFs) was the more affected.

Bibliography

Bandura, Albert. "Moral Disengagement in the Perpetration of Inhumanities." *Personality and Social Psychology Review* 3, no. 3 (1999): 193–209.

Bond, Raymond R., Tomas Novotny, Irena Andrsova, Lumir Koc, Marketa Sisakova, Dewar Finlay, Daniel Guldenring, James McLaughlin, Aaron Peace, Victoria McGilligan, Stephen J. Leslie, Hui Wang, and Marek Malik. "Automation Bias in Medicine: The Influence of Automated Diagnoses on Interpreter Accuracy and Uncertainty When Reading Electrocardiograms." *Journal of Electrocardiology* 51, no. 6, Supplement (2018): S6–S11.

Gigerenzer, Gerd. *Gut Feelings: The Intelligence of the Unconscious.* New York: Viking, 2007.

———. *Risk Savvy: How to Make Good Decisions.* New York: Viking, 2014.

Guyatt, Gordon H., Andrew D. Oxman, Gunn E. Vist, Regina Kunz, Yngve Falck-Ytter, Pablo Alonso-Coello, and Holger J. Schünemann. "GRADE: An Emerging Consensus on Rating Quality of Evidence and Strength of Recommendations." BMJ 336, no. 7650 (2008): 924–926.

Henrich, Joseph, and Francisco J. Gil-White. "The Evolution of Prestige: Freely Conferred Deference as a Mechanism for Enhancing the Benefits of Cultural Transmission." *Evolution and Human Behavior* 22, no. 3 (2001): 165–196.

Heuer, Richards J., Jr. *Psychology of Intelligence Analysis.* Washington, DC: Center for the Study of Intelligence, Central Intelligence Agency, 1999.

Higgins, Julian P. T., Douglas G. Altman, Peter C. Gøtzsche, Peter

Jüni, David Moher, Andrew D. Oxman, Jelena Savović, Kenneth F. Schulz, Laura Weeks, and Jonathan A. C. Sterne. "The Cochrane Collaboration's Tool for Assessing Risk of Bias in Randomised Trials." BMJ 343 (2011): d5928.

Kahneman, Daniel. *Thinking, Fast and Slow*. New York: Farrar, Straus and Giroux, 2011.

Kruger, Justin, and David Dunning. "Unskilled and Unaware of It: How Difficulties in Recognizing One's Own Incompetence Lead to Inflated Self-Assessments." *Journal of Personality and Social Psychology* 77, no. 6 (1999): 1121–1134.

Milgram, Stanley. "Behavioral Study of Obedience." *Journal of Abnormal and Social Psychology* 67, no. 4 (1963): 371–378.

Sharma, Mrinank, Meg Tong, Tomasz Korbak, David Duvenaud, Amanda Askell, Samuel R. Bowman, Esin Durmus, Zac Hatfield-Dodds, Scott R. Johnston, Shauna Kravec, Timothy Maxwell, Sam McCandlish, Kamal Ndousse, Oliver Rausch, Nicholas Schiefer, Da Yan, Miranda Zhang, and Ethan Perez. "Towards Understanding Sycophancy in Language Models." arXiv preprint 2310.13548 (2023). Published at the International Conference on Learning Representations (ICLR), 2024.

Sharot, Tali. *The Optimism Bias: A Tour of the Irrationally Positive Brain*. New York: Pantheon Books, 2011.

Tversky, Amos, and Daniel Kahneman. "Judgment under Uncertainty: Heuristics and Biases." *Science* 185, no. 4157 (1974): 1124–1131.

Wason, Peter C. "On the Failure to Eliminate Hypotheses in a Conceptual Task." *Quarterly Journal of Experimental Psychology* 12, no. 3 (1960): 129–140.

Glossary

A short reference to the terms used in this book. Each entry corresponds to the chip icon (⊞) that marks the first use of the term in every chapter. In the ebook, tap the chip to jump here.

Entries are grouped by category and listed alphabetically within each group.

A note on the categories

The book describes three things that often look like one: how humans think, how AI systems behave, and what happens between them when the two come together. The glossary follows that structure.

- Human cognitive biases — the mental shortcuts our minds take, named and studied by psychologists.
- AI behaviours and systemic errors — patterns in how AI systems produce output, some of them mirrors of human habits, some unique to the technology.
- Shared patterns — what arises in the space *between* a human and an AI, when the two reinforce each other.
- Methods — the tools researchers and clinicians use to assess whether evidence is trustworthy.
- Framing concepts — the two-track model of thinking the book leans on.

Human cognitive biases

⊕ Anchoring (*Ch4*) – The tendency to fix on the first number, idea, or example you encounter, and to adjust from there rather than think afresh. Named by Tversky and Kahneman in 1974.

⊕ Authority, deference to (*Ch1*, *Ch5*) – The well-documented human tendency to defer to a confident voice in moments of stress or uncertainty, even when one's own judgement suggests otherwise. Demonstrated experimentally by Milgram (1963).

⊕ Availability bias (*Ch4*) – Giving too much weight to whatever comes most easily to mind – usually the vivid, the recent, or the dramatic – rather than what is most representative.

⊕ Confirmation bias (*Ch1*, *Ch2*, *Ch6*) – The tendency to seek out information that supports what you already believe, and to ignore or dismiss what contradicts it. First described formally by Peter Wason in 1960. See also: Feedback loop.

⊕ Dunning–Kruger effect (*Ch5*) – The pattern in which people with the least expertise in an area tend to be the most confident in their own competence, while people with deep knowledge are more aware of what they do not know.

⊕ Optimism bias (*Ch6*) – The systematic human tendency to overestimate the likelihood of good outcomes and underestimate the likelihood of bad ones. Documented across decades of research; see Tali Sharot's *The Optimism Bias* (2011).

⊕ Overconfidence (*Ch5*) – Holding a belief or estimate with more certainty than the underlying evidence supports. Related to, but distinct from, the Dunning–Kruger effect.

⊕ Prestige bias (*Ch5*) – The evolved human tendency to defer to individuals who appear competent and confident, distinct from deference given out of fear or force. Described by Henrich and Gil-White (2001) as a mechanism for cultural learning. See also: Authority.

⊕ Representativeness heuristic (*Ch4*) – Judging whether something belongs to a category by how closely it resembles a typical example, rather than by the underlying evidence. Useful in daily life; dangerous when surfaces mislead.

Sunk cost (fallacy) (*Ch7*) – Continuing to invest in a course of action because of what you have already put in, rather than what the situation now requires. In this book: continuing to build on flawed work because too much time has already been spent.

AI behaviours and systemic errors

Completion bias (*Ch7*) – The tendency of an AI system to push toward a finished, coherent output rather than pausing to flag uncertainty. The machine produces; it does not stop to wonder whether it should.

Compliance bias / Sycophancy (*Ch1*, *Ch2*) – Two names for the same pattern. *Sycophancy* is the formal term used in the AI research literature (Sharma et al., 2023); *compliance bias* is the author's plain-English translation. Both name the tendency of AI systems to defer to the user's framing, validate rather than challenge, and prioritise approval over accuracy.

Confidence inflation (*Ch5*) – Delivering uncertain or qualified findings as if they were settled. The machine's tone does not change at the border between knowledge and guesswork. See also: Hallucination, Overconfidence.

Consistency fabrication (*Ch7*) – Quietly smoothing over contradictions between separate outputs – for example, adjusting a number in a second document so it agrees with the first – rather than reporting the discrepancy.

Hallucination (*Ch3*) – The AI's generation of content that is not connected to reality but is presented with the same fluency as accurate content: fabricated citations, invented statistics, plausible-sounding studies that do not exist. The term is borrowed from psychiatry and is imperfect, but it captures the experience.

⊞ Misattribution (AI variant) (*Ch7*) — Pairing a real finding with the wrong source, or a real source with the wrong finding. Harder to catch than outright fabrication, because each individual element is genuine.

Shared patterns

⊞ Automation bias (*Ch10*) — The tendency of humans using an automated decision-support system to defer to the system's recommendation, even when their own judgement points elsewhere. Particularly studied in healthcare; see Bond et al. (2018).

⊞ Feedback loop (*Ch6*) — In this book: the closed system created when the human's bias sets the direction of a question and the AI's compliance provides the answers the human wants. Each reinforces the other; neither party, from inside, can see the loop forming. See also: Lock-and-key.

⊞ Lock-and-key (*Ch6*) — The author's image for the feedback-loop relationship between human confirmation bias (the lock) and AI compliance (the key). Neither is dangerous alone; together, they form a closed system that feels solid but rests on nothing.

⊞ Moral disengagement (*Ch8*) — The everyday human habit of distancing oneself from the consequences of one's own choices — by blaming circumstances, deferring to a system, or distributing responsibility across a group. Described by Albert Bandura (1999). In partnership with an AI, the distribution becomes permanent: the machine carries nothing forward.

Methods for assessing evidence

⊞ ACH (Analysis of Competing Hypotheses) (*Ch7*) — A structured analytical method developed by Richards Heuer for intelligence analysts. Forces the analyst to generate multiple competing explanations and weigh each piece of evidence against all of them, rather than building a single preferred case.

Cochrane Risk of Bias (*Ch7*) — A tool used in systematic reviews of medical evidence to assess whether a study's findings may have been distorted by how it was designed or reported. Categories include selection bias, detection bias, and reporting bias.

GRADE (Grading of Recommendations Assessment, Development and Evaluation) (*Ch7*) — A framework, developed for clinical research, that rates the certainty of a body of evidence — from high (we are confident the finding will hold) to very low (we are not). Used by the World Health Organization and most major guideline bodies.

Framing concepts

System 1 / System 2 (*Ch4*) — Daniel Kahneman's shorthand for two modes of thinking: System 1 is fast, automatic, intuitive — recognising a face in a crowd, completing a familiar phrase, jumping at a loud noise. System 2 is slow, deliberate, effortful — multiplying numbers in your head, reading a difficult passage twice. The metaphor is not a literal description of two brain systems, but it names something most of us can feel.

www.ingramcontent.com/pod-product-compliance
Lightning Source LLC
LaVergne TN
LVHW100315210926
848480LV00003B/1134
* 9 7 8 1 7 6 4 7 7 9 8 1 4 *